Judging Hope

Judging Hope

A Reach to the True and the False
Michael Gelven

St. Augustine's Press
South Bend, Indiana

Manufactured in the United States of America.

1 2 3 4 5 6   25 24 23 22 21 20 19

Library of Congress Control Number: 2020933720

∞ The paper used in this publication meets the minimum requirements of the American National Standard for Information Sciences – Permanence of Paper for Printed Materials, ANSI Z39.48-1984.

St. Augustine's Press
www.staugustine.net

TABLE OF CONTENTS

CHAPTER ONE | The Question

Lasciate ogni speranza, voi ch'entrate
"Abandon hope all ye who enter here." (Carey Translation)

'These words, according to the poet Dante, are inscribed above the entrance to hell. It is the supreme moment in the current of human reading; it chills and stuns with its truth. Hell for the medieval Christian is absolute failure, the only radical and total loss we can conceive, and in spite of its fires and torments that so vividly enliven this great Italian epic, its essence—abandoning hope—tortures more than the meted sanction to any specific sinner there. The opposite of hope is often thought as despair, and even the modern disbeliever can sense the terror of this; death itself seems far less bleak than endless, crushing nihilism, eclipsing all worth, leaving us feckless beggars for the only alms that matter yet never come: the coins that purchase oblivion.

Yet even this magnificent poetic line is ambiguous. Is it a mere factual claim: there is no hope in hell? Is it a final, prudent warning? Leave hope behind, for if you bring it in with you the torment will be worse? If you can learn to abandon any expectation of delivery, your timeless anguish will be muted; dullness and apathy are the only narcotics here. If the inscription were to mean there is no hope in hell, the greatest pang would be lost. Without hope there is no disappointment, no frustration at the unachieved, no sense of thwarted victory. A theological sadist might say: keep hoping, damned soul, for if you anaesthetize that yearning your aching sleeps, and I would have you awake to suffer more. The epic artist may be suggesting the inversion: hope abandons you when you enter here. Poets are an envied lot: they say one thing and mean many; all three of these readings may be contained, for the truth in each adds to the enormity of the line. There is no proscription against poets doing what is denied the rest of us: we find it artful to let them cast out single lines that snag many fish. Even so, the reader is loath to surrender the power of that one word, Lasciate, abandon or leave. To be abandoned is to be left alone, marooned on a desolate isle or unreachable wasteland, exiled from all warmth and sharing; not merely executed in the public square where fellow townsmen gather as companions to our departure. It is no accident that the pit of this poet's inferno is not fire but a frozen lake, cut off by icy distance; nor is it inapt to find there those who betray, for betrayal is a species of exile: we cut off all ligatures that enable belonging. We betray only our friends. This is a species of abandonment that itself abandons.

But what is it that we abandon, or by which we are abandoned? Is not hope merely a futural wish? This seems heaven, not hell. No longer to need to wish—what could be a greater boon? Or if it be a loss, how trivial it seems, for an avid youth may plant a hundred wishes each day, and even if all wither, his morrow is blessed by unasked boons. This surely is not the stuff of greatness; no epic is wrought on such a slender reed as wishing for a future favor. But if, by hope, we mean more than a mere futural wish, then the present task is a weighty one indeed. If the abandonment of hope is hell, then hope matters far beyond a mere desire for future benefits; indeed it is beyond all desire whatsoever. Despair is no mere disappointment; it is mockery to suggest so profound a darkness is the mere frustration of desire. But if hope is the counter of despair, it too is mocked by seeing it as a mere optimistic anticipation that things will go our way. Hope conceived as a trust in a felicitous future equates with naiveté or childish romanticism. Indeed, so conceived, the dire imperative over Dante's portal to hell could be transported to the portal of heaven: abandon hope all who enter the shining gates, for here you do not need to hope, since all is given. As far as hope is concerned, there is no difference between heaven and hell; it is lacking in both.

This equation does not trouble too much, since the easy rejoinder is so ready: hope means more than wishing for a happy future. It is precisely this ready move, however, that snarls our clarity. What, then, can hope possibly mean? If it is not an interior pep talk to keep us from spiritual defeat before the battle is actually waged, what could it mean? Our literary history ranks it rather highly. It is the final Greek refugee from Pandora's box, it ranks with faith and love in Paul's famous trilogy, it is the solution to the first of the three riddles given to Calaf by the icy Princess, Turandot, in

Puccini's opera; for our early British colonists America was "the hope of the world." Emily Dickinson says it is the thing with feathers that perches in the soul. It is, perhaps, a species of mockery to pass over such a list; perhaps part of our mistake in confronting all great themes is to hurry past these literary resources as if they were mere sentiments to lush a dreamy mind.

Consider for example what happens to the apparent mawkish and sentimental banality of the first line when the great poet continues:

"Hope" is the thing with feathers
That perches in the soul,
And sings the tune without the words,
And never stops at all,

And sweetest in the Gale is heard;
And sore must be the storm
That could abash the little Bird
That kept so many warm.

I've heard it in the chillest land,
And on the strangest sea;
Yet, never, in extremity,
It asked a crumb of me. (#254 Johnson)

What begins as an almost childish bit of fluff, nearly embarrassing us with its sugary, girlish naiveté, becomes in a tenure of twenty seconds a source of awe. Two lines stand out: what does it mean to say hope "sings the tune without the words"? And what does it mean to say that hope "never, in extremity, asked a crumb of me?" Perhaps to sing the tune of hope without the words is to say hope is elusive of propositional form; or that it comes to us as a feeling, not as a message, or even that to put it into words disenables its efficacy. Or is it a simple parallel: just as much music is without words yet still moves us powerfully with specific passions, so hope need not be expressed in order to be felt. Words are always within a specific language, such as English or German, but the German Mozart transcends even European boundaries, and is revered in China and Japan. The image of singing the tune without words thus suggests a universality beyond the local. The last line is richly ambivalent: it could mean that she, the poet, has never in her extremities been offered the crumb of hope: she, profound realist as she is, was never offered hope's crutch; she had to limp through her storms and gales unaided by its blessing. Relying, as she does, on the word and not the word-less tune, she would not share her lonely strength with this comforting knot of feathers. Yet, the same line also suggests an opposite reading: hope gives without payment. It has never asked even of her the tiniest crumb in recompense. Like a doting parent, hope simply gives, inexhaustibly. It is a curiosity that, for all its bestowal, hope itself is never thanked. Dickinson forces us to face this shameless abundance: no poet, not even she, thanks hope. We might thank God or the stars or the serendipity of evolution, or our training that gives us courage, but hope, whether personified or abstracted, seems incapable of being thanked. Is there some buried jewel of wisdom in this? She certainly teases us with the suggestion. Are we deeply flawed in being unable to thank the thing with feathers? Or can hope be called this anymore? If not, this may explain why she puts hope in double quotes—something she rarely does?

Lest it seem the reading here is forced, we must remember the quality and stature of this poet; she has written further on the theme:

Hope is a subtle Glutton;
He feeds upon the fair;
And yet, inspected closely,
What abstinence is there!

His is the halcyon table
That never seats but one,
And whatsoever is consumed
The same amounts remain.

Here the word is not in double quotes; here the image is darker and elusive; here there is no suggestion of bawdy sentiment. Each pair of lines is an anomaly: we hear conflicting messages. One reading of the first pair is that when we hope we are like gluttons feeding on what is hoped for: the fair. Or we can also hear the opposite: we are the fair ones on whom the glutton, as some externalist influence, feeds—we are the prey of the predator, hope. The term 'Abstinence' in the second pair thus becomes either the emptiness that follows from feeding on what offers no real sustenance, or it becomes the Lenten restraint of the externalist force that does not truly devour us. The halcyon table suggests hope is a beneficial host—yet "halcyon" also hints of dissembling nostalgia, evoking memories of youth from the filter of distance. The deeper puzzle is why the table seats but one. Does this mean those who hope are isolated, set apart because others have while they only yearn? Or does it mean that hope is the only table we have when in distress? Are we isolated, or is hope itself isolated? Is hope the host who dines alone without guests—leaving us unfed? The final pair of lines echoes the second pair: if the same amount remains are we to believe that hope is endless in its resource and sustaining power, or does the line again suggest that the food of hope has no nutrition? With this poet there is no single rendering; we must hear the conflicts: the rich, almost impressionistic imagery surprises by its power to move us to a wondrous bewilderment. These multiple meanings do not offer the reader options, as if we could interpret the poem as we like: rather, they all must be accepted at once. It is difficult to imagine any honest reader who is not addled by this poem; at the same time, however, we are loathe to leave its promise. Perhaps it is reflexive in the sense that the experience of reading the poem is akin to the experience of hope: true hope confuses, too. At the very least she of Amherst has shown there is a darker side to hope. How can hope darken?

One way to glimpse this darkness—or at least the shadows cast if hope be like the sun—is to reflect on whom it sustains darkly. To paraphrase George B. Shaw: He who can, does; he who cannot, hopes. To rely exclusively on hope suborns the will to act; the more fiercely we screw our energies to the adhesive sticking of hope, the less we rely upon our power to extricate ourselves from peril by action. Not all who hope yield in this way; we may even suggest rightly that hope companions effort or even enables it—that mere hope alone is dark. Perhaps this is a deeper reading of why hope dines alone: Hope by itself is dark; hope only as a prop to action lightens.

The suggestion that hope unlinked to action need always be dark cannot be left unchallenged, even though there is surely some truth in the realization that mere hoping may be a narcotic against the will to extricate oneself from peril and the lethargy that keeps us there. Hope, even if un-coupled to action, need not always darken. We can imagine two people: one so favored by fortune there is little spur to hope at all; the other, ill-favored by circumstances, who must hope fiercely and often even to survive. It is quite possible that the former, not needing hope, accepts the pleasantness of an unchallenged life without gratitude, and drifts along with equanimity; whereas the latter, in the very act of hoping, becomes a nobler soul, more dependent on the powers within, and all the more grateful for whatever crumbs of favor may rarely occur. One might, with this consideration, deem the first less virtuous than the second; and such judgment seems to entail that hope itself can then be a virtue. Here the problem itself is brought into sharper focus by the paradox. Hope, especially if unlinked to action, appears both a vice and a virtue. Though it obviously can be a virtue, it is the pos-sibility it can be a vice that deepens our concern with its truth. The paradox now reveals its power to illuminate the deeper realization: perhaps only in the light of the dark—an anomalous phrase, to be sure—may we learn the truth that lurks beneath these myriad judgments about hope. Perhaps there is, beneath these multiple meanings, an underlying reality which may be called "fundamental hope." One goal of this inquiry would be to isolate, if possible, this fundamental understanding that enables all the others, recog-nizing that the truth of hope may offer itself only in the elusive.

Riddles certainly are elusive. The Princess Turandot offers Calaf the first riddle:

Nella cupa notte vola un fantasma iridescente.
In the dark of night flies an irridescent Phantom

Sale e spiega l'ale
Soaring and spreading its wings

Sulla nera infinita umanita
Above the black infinity of humanity

Tutto il mundo l'invoca
All in the world call on it

e tutto il mundo l'implora
And all in the world implore it.

Ma il fantasma sparisce coll'aurora
But the phantom vanishes at dawn

Per rinascere nel cuore
to be born again in the heart

Ed ogni notte nasce
At each night it is born

Ed ogni giorno muore!
At each day it dies!

That Calaf correctly interprets this as hope cheats us of the riddle. How many of us would be able to untangle the royal hint properly? I doubt I could; but knowing the answer makes it seem obvious.

It is, however, a rather bleak account, suggesting hope is a mere illusion—the stuff of nightly dreams that vanishes with the dawn. This is her account of hope as a deceit: it promises but never yields. Note her depiction of us: nera infinita umanita—the black infinite humanity—over which a mere ghost—fantasma—flies only when we are in the illusion of dreams. Not for the icy, distant princess is there any hope for the hopeful. The answers to the next two riddles are blood, and Turandot herself, suggesting the course of the whole drama: hope, the great betrayer, lures the fool to his bloody death. Yet Calaf, in conquering the first two wins the third; but not without dire cost: Liu, the sweet girl empowered by love to huge courage is tortured and dies. It is not a pretty story, even in its success. Perhaps the sheer romanticism of the opera deceives us: hope is exactly as Turandot describes: its beneficence is deceptive. Yet what is inescapable in this concrete instance offered by art is this: hope is, was, and remains a riddle, indeed a riddle that if left unfaced, is dire.

These literary passages serve to remind us that hope is elusive even as it is more serious than mere idle dreaming. The philosopher, however, wants at least to know the genus. If it is not a mere wish or idle dream, to what class or category does it belong? Is it a virtue? A faculty? A psychological feeling or act? In one of the more remarkable of his many remarkables, Kant tells us there are three interests of reason: what can I know? What ought I to do? What may I hope? To rank hope with moral action and reliable knowledge as constituting one third of reason's interests may be the most exaggerated instance of hoping ever suggested. Is hope a part of reason, just as knowledge and morality are? It is not immediately clear what it means to say reason has interests at all, but to suggest hope is a fundamental one seems to alter everything we normally think about when considering reason. This is holy territory for the philosopher, and Kant, as the supreme critic or high priest of reason, is loath to let anything into this sacred precinct without first passing the most rigorous of initiatory rites. Yet hope seems to pop up without any warning or preparation in the final section of the *Critique of Pure Reason* called the "Canon." His argument is there however, at least in hybrid form, and once made, the suggestion cannot be easily dismissed: is the proper genus for hope the very nature of reason itself? Must a reasoner hope?

To shift from the literary and philosophical to the theological may further our bewilderment and our learning. Many Christian thinkers argue that if there is such a thing as an unforgivable sin it is the second sin against hope, despair; the first sin against hope is presumption, which apparently can be forgiven. Why do these theologians say this?

Certainly they cannot mean by "despair" these passing moods into which all of us descend from time to time that render us dismally pessimistic or even nihilistic, for if these moods are unforgivable sins then we are all damned. It would seem, then, that unforgivable despair is a deeply-rooted, willful, sustained rejection of all possible hope, and not the mere circumstantial condition of lacking actual hope. Let us assume provisionally these theologians are correct: anti-hope (despair) would be a sin; this implies that hope itself is a theological (as opposed to a mere practical) virtue. Hope would then be a result of a free will or at least of a responsible agent: it could even be an act, and indeed an act at which we can either succeed or fail. If failing at it damns us, it would seem to be more than a simple act of the moment; such failure would be sustained, character-changing, and a developmental ruination of the soul. Success, on the other hand, would itself be a mighty endeavor, for as an accomplishment it enables our redemption. From Dickinson's little feathered thing to the theologian's massive necessity seems a rather wide distance. The poet speaks in a whisper, the theologian roars with a shout; can they possibly be speaking of the same thing? Can the poet and theologian serve as resources for the philosopher's linking hope with our ability to reason at all?

From certain critical perspectives these prior paragraphs may seem wild; perhaps even surpassing wild to frenzy. How could hope enable redemption since redemption itself is rank superstition? If believing in hope makes you feel good, okay; but don't bring it into the classroom or write it on a public page or air it on accessible airwaves. Take it like Prozac perhaps, but do not link it at all to knowledge, truth, or reason. Prozac is hope in a bottle; it works solely as a chemical reaction in the brain, and such an account alone is reliable. Aside from the chemical reaction, hope is a mere sentiment, and as such, Dickinson's first sugary line is enough. Prozac is a thing with feathers, perched upon the brain.

There is much that attracts in this gruff but practical mistrust. Cheap sentiment is unworthy for a truth-seeker, and a healthy disdain for the bawdy hucksters of license and anthropomorphic nostrums may be our finest immunity against banality. One need not be an extremist in such mistrust to take alarm at profligacy. Perhaps this array of poet, composer, philosopher, and theologian is a species of overkill. They all speak loftily of hope, but do they explain it? Perhaps there is more to hope than an antidepressant chemical, but as thinkers, a certain robust critique is essential if we are to learn. Certainly if a starry-eyed romantic and optimist is the paradigm of one who hopes, then a healthy scowl from a tougher mind seems in order. Even the toughest of these must pause at the array suggested: Kant and Paul and Dante and Dickinson are themselves tough; they are not easily persuaded by sheer sentiment nor do they lack the penetrative power of the deepest thinkers. Kant gives us an argument, not a mere idle remark. Perhaps a brief reflection on his reasoning may give us purchase on this elusive notion. He says something like this:

Human experience tells us that in the actual world there are unanswered wrongs—i.e., injustice. The moral law tells us we ought not to wrong another; and our concern for justice tells us that those who do wrong to others should be punished; perhaps we even need to suggest that the victims—those who are wronged—in some sense should be provided with off-setting recompense. Reason itself demands that the various faculties must ultimately be able to be synthesized, so that what we learn through our senses ultimately must conform to what is demanded by the principles of the understanding. This synthesis is needed even in cognition: when I see someone push the switch and then see the light go out, the constancy of that connection at least suggests there is a principle—in this case the causal principle—that makes the connection thinkable rather than merely observable. When we observe that evil-doers are not punished and honorable people are often victims, we become aware of a discord between the faculties. We see what ought not to be the case. To be able to do wrong is grounded in our freedom, and as such may be too precious to surrender; but justice also matters. What I cannot will as a universal law is immoral; and I cannot will that there be radically unanswered wrongs. From experience, however, I know as a fact that in this earthly world there are unanswered and unanswerable wrongs. This, then, is the dilemma: what must we, as reasoners, think?

Reason, by itself, is prohibited from proving the existence of anything. It cannot prove the existence of rain, since a world without rain is logically possible. I am assured of rain only by my experiencing it. Thus it is not surprising that reason, by itself, since it cannot prove the existence of anything, does not prove the existence of souls or God. Reason can, however, provide rules by which we think, among which is the moral law governing conduct. However, reason also demands an ultimate synthesis of the various ways we think, along with the faculties that enable such thinking. Given that our actual, experienced world does not provide this unity, we must be able to consider the possibility of a world that does; that is: we must postulate such a possibility. A soul that endures past our present state may thus be postulated, for only if there is such a soul that is enabled to reach beyond the justice-deficient actual world, can I even imagine how to link this world of actual moral judgments—including the judgment that I cannot will unanswered wrongs—to the actual occurrence in this world of unanswered wrongs. I must synthesize these two faculties demanded by reason's need for possible completeness or unity. To postulate such a soul is ... hope—or to be more precise, it is rational hope.

This is, to be sure, a surface sketch. Many find in it a mere idle fantasy, a species of "pie-in-the-sky" naiveté. It may be many things, but it is not naiveté. It may be vulnerable to criticism—what philosophical argument is not?—but it is not an idle argument. Indeed, those who dismiss it with a cavalier smirk are just as naive as those who assume it proves the existence of a theistic god. The argument needs further critique; it is sketched here to show what Kant means by linking hope to our ability to reason. Consider the deeper issue that lurks behind the argument. Were we, as reasoners, bereft of hope in this transcendental sense, there would be no connection or synthesis between three capital faculties: that which enables us to think about injustice; that which enables us to think morally; and that which enables us to learn from experience. We would have only these independent faculties, floating unanchored to each other or to a unifying bedrock in a harbor. I would see injustice, know it was wrong, and realize it deserved censure; but there would be no rational basis for making sense of being the same mind that does each of these things; they would be radically disjoined. I could be reasonable within each area of thought but I could not be reasonable about thinking them in light of each other. For Kant, such radical disjunction of the faculties is an offense to what it means to reason at all. The point that emerges is this: to assume there must be some connection among our various faculties is not a mere entertainment of the possibility of another mental act, hoping; rather the reflection on this need is hope itself; or to put it more precisely: to reflect on the need for coherence among the faculties is to hope. That is a remarkable claim; it deserves our thinking.

Kant is not the only philosopher who thinks deeply about hope, any more than Dickinson is the only poet who illuminates its essence, or Puccini the only composer who confronts it musically. The nature of this initial chapter forfeits any suggestion of a hint as to how to resolve what is only now emerging as a question. We must survey the entire estate before we can lay claim to the landscape, much less establish ownership or sovereignty over it. There are other acres that must be tilled—other voices that must be heard; and among them are historians. It was not only the stern preacher in colonial America who thought of the new land as the hope of the world; it was the vast majority of these hardy settlers who deemed it so. What did they mean? Are there remnants even now at the new millennium that echo this audacious judgment? Is this loud, arrogant, venal, trashy and mercantile giant, this self-centered and vulgar superpower, in any sense at all a hope?

How can a nation be a hope? Historians can be just as guilty of excess as poets, philosophers, and opera composers; they can also be, as revisionists, just as mean-spirited, misanthropic, and skeptical. America, they say, either with cynical contempt or with a little awe, is the land of hope; it is the supreme polity for opportunity, the last bastion of merit. Even the poorest, lowest, most despised by caste, race, or religion, can achieve greatness here; even the angels here have hand-guns and bad debts and horrible habits of consuming the toxins of popular culture. But—

The land of merit and opportunity is not the same as the hope of the world. Opportunity and hope are not interchangeable. If the early colonists as well as the nineteenth century critics meant anything in their perception of America as the hope of the world, they did not mean simply that here one has opportunity. Hope meant rather a source of light, a beacon, a guide. These were sharp-minded men, hugely mistrustful of human folly; they certainly did not believe or even suggest that this then-fair (meaning "lovely") land sheltered only saints or heroes. Their constitution was filled with many checks and balances just because they knew power corrupts and that all of us, particularly those who aspire to govern, are weak. Yet, with all this palpable mistrust, sometimes bordering on misanthropy, they still thought of this as the land of hope. What they meant by this is really rather simple and direct: America ennobles its citizens, and indirectly, the whole earth. Hope here is not some futural wish, not even is it the promise of redemption; it is a way of being, an inheritance or bestowal, that makes us nobler—more splendid—creatures. It was seen as the hope of the world because the "old" world—Europe—was seen as base. America was not merely a place, but a way of being. What England called its liberties America called its inalienable rights, thereby grounding its success not in itself but in what was beyond itself. They held their truths to be self-evident: any human mind is capable of grasping the absolutely secure realization that the governed matter more than those who govern. So, in a great paradox, only in this particular land could one achieve the universal truth that all of us are free by nature. That paradox is still with us. That paradox is America. That paradox is hope.

For the early Americans, hope was a paradigm and a paradox; a way of being which ennobles. Like a rapidly growing child, the word seems to outgrow its clothing even as we watch it. Many terms have contextual diversities that require lengthening their columns in dictionaries; is this what is happening here? Or is it possible that the contributions of the literary, the theological, the philosophical, and the historical are not of specialized subsets, but of the same thing? With an idea as complex and as rich as hope, the first—but not the only—danger is to approach the inquiry without seeing the full range of its possibilities. It may seem at first that calling on these various voices gravely complicates the issue; but on reflection it actually enables the inquiry, and renders it available to thought.

Bromides, however, do not enable but usurp thought. "Where there's life, there's hope." This apparently is a prop to optimism: as long as we are alive it is possible that things might turn out in our favor. We know a few stories in which one who had despaired of salvation or extrication from the dire had, at the last moment, been granted a reprieve which then proved beneficial, offering a happy ending to his story. Since this can happen, we are told, we ought not ever give up. There is, of course, nothing wrong with reminding those in distress that things may turn out well; we do not want to discourage those who may yet, with some further effort, achieve success. But if this bit of prudence is meant as some profound insight into natural destiny, the adage deceives. First, as a claim it is simply false: not all who live do hope. Further, the number of those who hope yet fail may be far greater than those who hope and win. Further yet, there is such a thing as false hope, the provocation of which may be genuinely cruel. It is not at all a worthy thing to tell a spine-damaged child that if he but hopes or prays enough he will walk; for then his failure to walk burdens by rendering it his responsibility: he did not hope enough; his continued paralysis is punishment for hoping too weakly. The greater courage of learning to live nobly—even splendidly—with the affliction may be blocked by the ill-advised hoping for the miraculous.

This dip into the bromide is of supreme philosophical import because it allows for the emergence of a central truth: there can be false hope. A false hope is not a hope that is unfulfilled, but a hope that is groundless and hence debasing. It is, if we like to be clever, hopeless hoping. Hopeless hoping may lead us to despair. It may seem ironic that it is the bromide, and not the philosopher or poet, that provides the first possible purchase on thinking about this phenomenon. Where to begin? With the realization of the difference between true hope and false hope. Where else should any thinker begin other than with the true and the false?

CHAPTER TWO | The False

The young father refused to accept the doctor's assurance that his infant son would not live beyond a few more months. Intelligent, he grasped the science; he knew the pathology of the illness, knew it was fatal. But overwhelmed with unexpected tenderness and spectacular love, he coupled his hope to prayer, creating an awesome faith in miracle. The infant was radiantly beautiful, with long lashes and a crown of golden curls that sweetened an already angelic face. The distraught father would spend his nights in half-sleep, cuddling the precious off-spring on his beating heart as if his own health could transfer through the rhythms into the small and fading life. Ceaselessly the parent couched his hope in prayer, convinced by some strange syllogism that on the quantity and quality of his orisons alone lay the child's sole access to a future. So intense became his prayerful hope he felt the reality of a personal deity as a palpable presence; the sincerity of his trust kindled a fierce pair of fiery loves for his child and his God: only the dubiety of his own capacity to hope sufficiently plagued him. His God was too good, his child too worthy of existence to deny the miracle if only he but hoped deeply enough; the failure, an unendurable possibility, would fall on him alone. Were he to hope too weakly, he would deem himself the assassin of his child. A curious joy threaded the fabric of his distress, for all things that made up the weave of his hope were of the magnificent. What outranks the splendor of a miracle, of a personal God heeding a father's plea, of a sweet child deserving life, of a hope that transcends the grim predictability of medical science? He learned to hope magnificently.

She, however, though no less loving of their son, hoped in another way. Her boy, she feared would die; but what of her husband? She hoped not only for the miracle, but for the man, for she saw the danger in how he hoped. Would the boy's death cause the father to lose his faith? Would it be even worse: keeping his faith he must then hate himself for failing to hope on the level that would have ensured a miracle? She both feared and loved his extreme devotion; it was so noble yet so very perilous. Perhaps as he was intelligent, she was wise. Her hope, articulated in prayer—though not confined to it—included her husband's humanity, which in some sense seemed as unlikely to be saved as her son's life; for could he endure either a life of self-hatred for not hoping enough, or a life bereft or all hope and faith, the kind of life he now hated most: a selfish, naturalistic, spiritless nihilism? She hoped for his courage.

How should we judge these two differing species of hope? Does not the magnificence inherent in his suffice to rank it a worthy and noble thing? Our parlance offers the curious phrase "false hope," suggesting there must also be a true. But false hope is not false merely because the desired is not achieved, for then we would have to be prescient to hope truly; this would not be hope at all, but certitude. In the vernacular false hope usually means there is no ground or justification at all for any trust—that the hope brings far greater agony in the disappointment; it is a species of cruelty. By the same case, true hope is not true because the desired is achieved; rather it is true because in hoping we are sustained and encouraged in a manner that is based on a genuine possibility of success; true hope ironically prepares us to endure failure should it come.

Given these two parents' love, we should not be so cold as to deny them hope altogether: they will, and perhaps should, hope in any event. But given the lugubrious destiny of their woes, we must wonder whether one or the other, or both or neither, manifest true hope; perhaps both are false? Is it not the case that the greater the threat, the nobler the hope? History and legend thrill us with stories of courageous resistance against huge odds, suggesting that any hope is better than none, that those who surrender hope altogether seem craven and unworthy. Even if these high hopes are dashed we sense their inspiration. If any depicted figure seems magnificent in the triumph of his spirit over the omens of disaster, is it not the fierce and hapless father? By contrast, is not the mother's hope overly practical, skirting the pedantic? Don't hope too much, it may distress you? Such frail prudence seems mocked by the unfettered passion of the father's longing. At this first reading it may seem that, if we are to judge at all, the mother's hope is false because it is frail, the father's true because it is noble.

It is the pace that troubles; it seems an unmeasured judgment, indecent in its haste. The slower thought seems weightier. It is the vernacular that bids us pause: why "true" and "false"? If we were offered "inspiring" rather than "true," or "hesitant" rather than "false," we may be satisfied with this first, if hurried, judgment. But "true" is a sacred word to the thinker; it is by right the ultimate word. Is the father's hope true? Or is there too much cloud, too much self-deceit and dissembling in the father's contrivances to warrant the noble title? Weak praise mocks what it smiles on. Must we now, against the prior sentiments, make sterner judgment? The father's hope is false; the mother's hope is true.

By what galling license do we dare to witness this knouting of the young father's soul and judge his hope as false? Has not his suffering redeemed in high coinage the base tariff of this censure? Do we deem his hope as false because the boy dies? Or is it false merely because in hoping so intensely the father suffers more? Is not the spectacle itself too mixed with other matter? Is it really hope that is false, or faith? Or is not mere self-deception excused by love? Would we really want to say he should not or even ought not to have hoped so fiercely? This last suggestion seems shameful: must hope be true only if tepid? These hesitations, though understandable as pity, are unworthy. The endurance by the father deserves a nobler response than sentiment: only truth measures up to what he suffers; and the truth is: the father is false in his hope. It is false not because the boy dies, but because, as false, it distorts the genuine phenomenon. The act of hoping becomes a mere contest of the will, for even if we provisionally accept the bizarre theology as true, then either the boy's life was achieved by mental effort, or his death resulted from a deficit of mental effort. If the father's intensity of feeling is a cause, then it is not hope at all. Should the boy live it would not even be a miracle in the strictest sense, for if such huge psychological energy brings about the son's triumph over the disease, it is science; anyone capable of such intense concentration would be able to save anyone imperiled by the disease. That is how we understand the word "cause." At the grieved passing the father laments: I did not hope enough. How could he have hoped more? Do we measure hope by the amount of energy dispensed by the one who hopes? Then it would be the psychic energy, not hope, that saves the child. Is God like a huckster of cotton candy at a carnival? "The cone cost fifteen cents, kid. You only have twelve cents? Too bad, cheat at the next booth and come back with the dough, and I'll sell you the cone for fifteen cents?" Indeed, as the scenario unfolds, the whole sordid picture becomes a deceit; hope is not hope, God is not God, miracles are not miracles, responsibility is not responsibility, victory is defeat. Even triumph would have been a cheat. Were his son to live, would the father be grateful for a bestowed miracle, or would he now assume his own powers made him a worker of wonders? Yet, we cannot deny in some sense he still hopes, which is why we must call it false hope.

If hope does not bring with itself some assurance, then why hope at all? Is the mother's hope any better? She hoped her son would live, even if only a miracle could save him. Her hoping, though not assured as her husband's, prolonged her agony, intensified her suffering, put her on the rack of doubt that may also have tried her faith. Why call hers true if his is false? Yet the difference matters. The difference is huge. The difference, we learn, is fundamental.

In ordinary understanding we speak, quite correctly, of false hope as a source of unnecessary, perhaps even gratuitous, suffering. We do not assure a child his now deceased grandmother will visit soon: the thwarted expectations time after time are too cruel; and the child will learn of her death anyway, but in the most wretched way, for now he has lost all trust in those he must trust most deeply. Perhaps it is difficult for us to tell him she is gone; but if we cower, as he still waits, we are poltroons, inflicting unearned torment by our timidity. There is nothing deep in this: it is simply common sense. Why, though, call it false hope rather than bad hope? It is false because it is not true: that is—it is false as a false face is untrue, though it still be a face. There is a problem here that needs deeper analysis. For all his love, sacrifice, and perhaps even enviable faith, the stricken father falsely hopes. The mother's hope is true—that is, it is real hope, not illusory. The drama of the tortured father is complex, and some may argue that as an example it serves us ill, since it is possible that what is false may be his faith, or his prayer, or even his love rather than his hope. This complexity as we shall learn, though troubling, is a boon, not a burden, for to grasp the essence of what distinguishes true from false hope requires we confront it as it is, and not as an abstraction. Hope is never an isolated phenomenon; it is always entangled with other, kindred phenomena such as faith and love and simple courage. This mingling is not arbitrary; it is a necessity. As thinkers we must isolate hope from courage and love and faith; but the actual phenomena that must be studied are complex in their mingling, so it is methodologically flawed to begin as if we knew the differences. Romeo's passion for Juliet may be true love and not merely youthful lust, but without lust there would not be Romeo loving Juliet. We know the difference, at least in some sense, though we need not always know the demarcation. Hope may not be without faith and courage, but we know the difference, though here, too, we need not know the demarcation.

Perhaps the ordinary account of false hope reflects the deeper. We call it false hope because it deceives; and hence true hope is so called because it reveals. This suggestion allows us to make some distinctions that ease our anxiety. The tormented father can now be admired for the intensity of his devotion, his sacrificial loving, his courage, even for the depth of his faith; we censure him solely on the basis that he allows these virtues (we may provisionally call them that) to rest upon the unstable ground of self-deceit. The nature of this deceit is not based on the error of his judgment about the future, nor on a bad religion that teaches superstition, but on his own reality: his hope is false because it belies who he is, and thus to some extent what must be called his false being. His wife, who aches and cares and prays as well as he, never loses sight of her own truth: she may plea before some deity, but does not transplant that deity in the soil of her own intensity of will. She realizes, perhaps in her anguish for the first time, she is not the sole determiner of her destiny, that not even her deep faith in her God deceives her into thinking her prayers are any less prayerful simply because they are not answered. Because of the painful learning, she is able in her dreadful torment to care not only about herself and her son, but about her husband's self-destruction based on false hoping. She cares about both his and her humanity.

Nevertheless one might suspect that the villain in this piece is not false hope but false belief: what turns us away from the father's plight is the hideous theological doctrine that all who pray intensely enough will in fact be given what they ask for. This is, admittedly, a curious teaching: suppose I pray intensely for the damnation of souls who do not deserve it. Would that be granted? If one suggests that only worthy pleas are granted, the entire conviction is rendered tepid: the father's prayers for a miracle saving his son are unavailing not because his prayers lacked sufficient intensity but simply because the plea itself was unworthy. This is an easily held belief, but it is not worth much, for then hope and prayer are irrelevant: if the plea is worthy—that is, he ought to be cured—then we should not pray for his cure but demand it. If this were the case, hope would play no role at all, suggesting that if there is such a thing as false hope it can only occur in the realm of warped faith in a theistic divinity. This is patently untrue.

An atheistic, naturalist father, confronted with his infant son's impending death, can also hope falsely; in some ways this false hope can be seen as parallel to the theist's. If he but searches fiercely enough through the annals of on-going experimentation he may find some researcher who vanguards the discipline and knows the key of technological wizardry that would derail the disease. The father may even suspect his local laboratories have misdiagnosed, or missed a subtle clue. Were he but to invest more money and energy he may find the researcher; if his beloved boy dies it may be his moral fault in not searching diligently enough. Such forms of self-deception are weeds that choke off the crops in any metaphysics or religion, for the fault lies not in what we believe but in how we hope. Nevertheless, the shift away from the darker species of theism may offer purchase on an entirely different way of hoping falsely. It may be worth reflecting on this as a resource for deepening our understanding of what it means to hope truly.

Suppose the atheistic father, confounded by his deep and surprising love for his new-born but fatally doomed child, aches with unexpected longing for a cure. His trust in the metaphysics of naturalism puts him in the clutches of a sadistic self-torment. He believes utterly that his own suffering is nothing but a natural phenomenon, just as the misfirings within the entirely natural entity he calls his son is explicable by efficient causal events. To hope is inconsistent with what he knows is inevitable; yet the fact that he experiences certain strong emotional feelings that include the psychological or even purely biological phenomenon that is called hoping, cannot be denied. He is persuaded that his own anguish, then, is nothing but purely physical phenomena. He seeks refuge in this belief. His hoping is merely a natural event; he can do nothing about it, so why struggle? Granted some naturalist fathers may indeed find solace in the recognition that their pain is merely nerve endings reacting to mental stress; for some this solace may even become a narcotic. But for this father, the narcotic is unavailing. He cannot find solace in his metaphysics simply because his

love for his son entails a sense of worth and meaning that is not enabled by
what he believes is true. He may then find himself hating himself for hoping; he is even ashamed, for his hope seems a mockery of himself; he sees
it as a species of superstition; but the more he mocks his own shame the
deeper it grows, for his sweet, adorable, deserving child seems to demand,
in his peril, a care that is not consistent with the father's judging the worth
of the boy and the worth of his own torment as determined, natural events.
He deems his hoping as vile self-deceit, unworthy of his mind, yet he hopes
anyway, hating his hoping and hence himself. Might not this, too, be seen
as false hope?

These reflections on both fathers suggest that false hope is independent
of any specific belief about the metaphysical make-up of the world, and
that what makes hope false is to forget or deny that hope may be necessary
for our being persons altogether, and that perhaps being able to be persons
always makes up, in part, what it means to hope at all. False hopers are
therefore revealed as deficient in—though not necessarily entirely lacking
in—a vivid sense of their own being persons. The latent, unspecified argument seems to be emerging along these lines: in order to hope truly one
must be a person, i.e., only persons hope. To hope in a way that entails the
hoper to be a non-person or to become more than or less than a person
would then be false hope. Such false hoping would be a species of unsound
reasoning or self-deception. Perhaps, then, the issue can be resolved on
purely formal grounds: false hope is hoping for what is irrational; true hope
hopes for what is at least rationally possible. What renders the theistic
father's hope false is that his son's being cured by prayer is irrational; what
renders the atheistic father's hope false is the irrationality inherent in believing his son's death is only a natural event and also believing that his
son's death somehow matters more than is warranted by a mere natural
event. As attractive as this codicil to the suggestion may be, however, it is
inadequate, since it is not at all obvious that mere formal reasoning is all
that is meant by being persons.

The wife of the father who prayed for a miracle that depended on the
intensity of his hoping shares many of the same beliefs and fierce feelings
as her husband; but it is possible to suggest her hope is true while his is
false. If this is correct, the reason for it seems to be that her hopes remain
consistent with her being a person. This, however, threatens to become a

mere slogan or chant unless it is more deeply considered. There is also the danger of circularity: only persons hope; only hopers are persons. Both arcs of the circle may be true, but they cannot be used as the rational bases for each other. The present stage of the inquiry however is not even close to such formal precision; we have merely a suggestion that might be illuminated by judging the wife's hope as true because it is consistent with her being a person, and also because it is about persons as persons, not as magicians. In what way does she hope? If what is hoped for is the same in both the father and the mother, the difference must be in her mode or way of hoping. There is no reason at all to suggest that she loves her son less, or that her belief in their God is less, or even that she is more uncertain of miracles. It may be that, in her hoping, she loves her husband more than he loves her; for she seems to play no role in his frenzied praying, but she clearly worries about him. Both hope, in part, because of the dreadful loss and its subsequent suffering that they must endure if their hopes are not realized. Perhaps his hope is false just because he does not or cannot accept that loss; her hope is true because she must accept it. One might be tempted to argue that the key to the difference is courage: she has more of it than he. It may be true she is more courageous, but if so it is a courage rooted in her acceptance of herself as a human person. Though she may still believe in the possibility of a miracle, she knows miracles are beyond her agency; her courage however belongs and originates in her. We may even suspect that because he refuses to accept he cannot in some way control the outcome; she, realizing the danger for him, is able to hope truly. Watching him hope falsely teaches her to hope truly.

With this exciting discovery we enable a further insight. Perhaps true hope is true only when one realizes false hope is possible. If we think of hope as mere emotional feelings, there could be no true or false hope. Once the sufferer realizes that false hope is a genuine possibility, the resistance to it, or the courageous commitment to hope otherwise, is enabled; but this decision is itself not the result of mere feelings or emotions that intensify our wishes; hence true hope is true just because we are the agency that makes it true. The bereft father can be thus read in two ways: the enormity of his feelings eclipses entirely his control; or, he freely chooses to hope falsely. In the first case he is weak, in the second, he is immoral. Sensing her husband hopes falsely, the stricken mother resolves to hope truly; but indeed it is her resolve that makes her hope true. Perhaps she senses that her love for her dying son is nobler if she hopes truly; she would not disgrace this radiant affection by linking her hope to self-contempt or self-deceit. Hers is a true hope because truth is enabled by it; she is forced to embrace this because she sees in her husband a hope that is false. It now becomes gloriously imperative to call hers a true rather than a good hope, and his a false, rather than a bad, hope; and the reason for this imperative is that truth matters, and truth mattering is essential for us to be persons. True hope is not based on the truth of the futural belief, but on hoping in a way consistent with our existential truth: being who we are.

The possibility of false hope enables hope to be true. Were I unable to lose, there would be no race, for a race must have a winner and a loser. At this stage of the inquiry it is perhaps necessary to disengage from the original example. It is enough to suggest that, as persons, we can hope truly or falsely, and were such disjunction left unthought, we could not hope at all, though we could still have hope-like feelings. This disengagement itself may seem ill-advised, for whenever we hope it seems we must be hoping for some particular boon, and unless we substitute another example, the danger is that hoping will be without a hope, and hence misleading. It is possible, however, to speak of a hopeful person without specifying the particular item desired; more importantly it is possible to consider what it means to be able to hope truly and falsely without hoping for a specific boon. We are hoping beings, even if we are not at a given moment desiring a specific thing: hope is of our essence, just as we might consider ourselves rational beings even if at the moment we are not engaged in a specific act of reasoning. However, in the present stage of this reflection we are considering what it means to be a hoping being solely from the sparked discovery that we hope both falsely and truly. An analogy may help. Suppose I run in a race. If, however, for reasons of affection, I prefer my opponent to win, I could still run, but deliberately mute my pace; in which case, though running I could not race. If so, this would not be a race. My opponent, however, may think it a real race, and so he runs as fast as he can in order to win. Is he racing? Or do we say he is merely running and is beguiled into believing he races? If my not trying to win disenables the race, can he be said to race in a non-race? There is a modern inclination to say that if he believes he races, then indeed he does race. But if my slower pace beguiles or deceives—and surely we must say this—then, if he is deceived he must be deceived in his judgment that he truly races. His running to win is therefore insufficient of itself to warrant calling the event a true race; and if it is not a true race, then does he merely run, though he believes he races? Or, might we rather suggest he races falsely, though there is no moral indictment placed on him, since it is I who deceive and he who is deceived. That, however, is the point: no matter how sincere his belief or genuine his effort, no matter how authentic his delight in crossing the finish line before me, he has raced falsely simply because there is no true race. His conviction that he races, and his effort in trying to win do matter in some sense, so we cannot say he does not race at all, but merely runs; rather we might say he races falsely, in the sense he did not compete in a "real" or "true" race. This judgment is reinforced by reflecting on what it would mean if, after the "race" he learned I had not tried to win, and hence I did not race. His hurt would be worse than had he lost the race, for his intense effort during the race and his high joy after the race would be revealed as gross deceits; the taste of his victory would be as ashes in his mouth; there would be a double ignominy: not only would he believe he might have lost had I truly raced, he also feels betrayed. Why would I do such a thing, and let him know, except to deflate his triumph and belittle his worth? But we still might want to say he races rather than merely runs; my guile renders his a false racing, not a non-racing run.

By analogy, false hope is still hope. If, however, we now speak not of a specific act of hoping but of hope as an essential modality of our humanity, we must ask: can hope, conceived as a modality of our humanity, be true and false? The very nature of the analog suggests it must be; but the suggestion is vacant unless supplied with concrete reflection. To suggest hope is essential for our being persons would mean such a characteristic is necessary: I cannot be a person without being enabled by hope; but even if this be true, it would not necessarily follow that such fundamental hoping as a necessary characteristic always be true hoping. What would it mean to say I may be fundamentally hoping, falsely? Were it possible for me as a hoping person to exist in such a way so as to disenable grasping that as a person truth matters, and hence hoping truthfully also matters, my being a hoping person might render my hoping false but not being an entirely non-hoping being. Just as the beguiled racer races falsely because, unknown to him, there is no real race since his opponent only runs, so our hoping may be real but false, even when we are not hoping for a specific boon but are enabled to be persons because of hope. Such a way of being would itself be false since it would include being unable to grasp that to hope belongs to our essence. Nevertheless, these remarks take us far ahead of what the inquiry now warrants; they merely point to what must lie ahead. The danger is that speculation may outpace concrete reflection, always a dire lapse in philosophical inquiry.

To avoid this danger it may be helpful to return to the distraught father who hopes and prays for a miracle. Perhaps the second verb outranks the first. Is it not false prayer rather than false hope that misleads the tormented parent? Or perhaps the word 'and' functions in the sentence as an appositive rather than a mere conjunction, suggesting that the father hopes—that is to say, prays—for a miracle. Is prayer a species of hope, or is hope a species of prayer? In some senses prayer is hope. "He hasn't a prayer" just means he has no hope for success. In its supplicant modality which, along with gratitude, is the most often intended, prayer seems an articulation of hope grounded in theistic belief. But need it be? Perhaps the analogue of prayer is not hope but a mere request. When I ask a friend to join me for dinner I may hope he accepts, but the request is not the hope itself, for I may hope without asking, and, in some cases, I may ask without hoping, as when I ask out of politeness, knowing he cannot come, or even asking for political reasons but hoping he will not accept. Nevertheless, there is a sufficient linkage between supplicant praying and hoping that might throw light on the present issue if we ask: can there be false and true (supplicant) praying? A philosophical analysis of the phenomenon of praying need not entail the adoption of any theological belief.

What would it mean to pray falsely? The mode of the present inquiry suggests that false prayer is not prayer to an incorrectly conceived God, such that all members of religion A pray falsely and all members of religion B pray truly. Nor does prayer become false if what is asked for in the prayer is not forthcoming. Perhaps by false prayer we mean praying in a manner that is inconsistent with or disenables what it means to pray at all. The wretched father may not only hope falsely, he may also pray falsely. His conviction that all who pray ardently enough will be granted their request may be simply a false belief. Does the falsity of the belief account for his false prayer? Or is it rather that the observer feels uneasy at the father's frantic shoveling more fuel on the furnace of his urgency so that what he intensifies is not his prayerfulness but his raw longing? Perhaps the fierceness of his desire disenables both hope and prayer precisely because what is desired becomes more important than his status as supplicant. He prays, not as a finite person making a request, but as a usurper of agency beyond what is enabled by who he is. If miracles are possible they are so only because of a personal God, not because of the intensity of emotion conceived as a cause in the one who prays. Few would deny, I think, that stoking up the fires of passionate commitment can, in some cases, achieve remarkable, highly unlikely results; and the vernacular often refers to such achievement as a "miracle," in the metaphoric sense, intending no divine intervention at all.

Even in such cases, however, there is often the uneasy feeling that the intensity of effort has so profoundly changed the character of the agent that we wonder if the achievement is worth the distortion. We can become monsters under the influence of an unchecked will. Child athletes who achieve stardom at the expense of their childhood are sad indicators of this; so too are remarkable tyrants such as Hitler and Stalin. Is it fair, though, to compare the grieving father with Hitler?

Yes. And, no. In a way he does become a monster; though unlike Hitler not necessarily an evil one; he harms no one but himself. Yet, even though one might judge his act of the will to be grotesque, his is still a prayerful act. Akin to the runner who outruns the non-racer and thus races falsely, the father prays, but does so falsely. He prays because his appeal is still made to a personal God even though in the guile of self-deceit he replaces the divine with his own intense willing. He prays falsely because he hopes falsely. What then, has been added to the inquiry by using prayer as a lever to upend the stone of impenetrability blocking our ascent on the mountain path? To say we pray falsely is not merely to say we hope falsely; praying falsely seems easier to grasp because of the theological machinery that supports it. We say he prays falsely in part because we do not hear in his entreaty the addendum "... but thy will be done." To pray as supplicant is to entreat as a bestowal; false praying, however, is not an entreaty by one person to another, but an assumption of a commercial algorithm—that is, a procedure which, if followed, guarantees results. We insert our bank card into the ATM, push the right buttons, and cash in disgorged; we are simply deceived if we claim that in such activity we ask, plea, or pray for our cash; perhaps it is even a deceit to say we hope for the money. Technophobes may be so distrustful of the efficacy of such devices that they actually pray, in some sense, to the goddess of electronics that the thing will work, but we are more amused than instructed by these aberrations. Normally the procedure with the ATM is entirely without hope or prayer. Certainly neither is needed. Thus, to hope or pray cannot be the mere following of an algorithm; yet one species of false praying seems to consist of distorting a plea into an algorithm. We are enabled by this analogy to suggest false hope is akin to false prayer. It is not necessary for the critic to be a theist at all to learn from the analogy. The false and the true here have nothing to do with theological or even metaphysical claims; rather it has to do with hoping as an essential quality of being a person, such that both true and false hoping are possible—and only by realizing this can we understand what it means to hope at all. The analogy with prayer is made to recognize an isomorphism between the two kindred phenomena, hope and prayer, as being both true and false.

To suggest that hope is an essential part of our being persons is to say that if we do not understand what it means to hope we do not understand what it means to be a person. To suggest further that hope itself can be true and false is to say we cannot understand the nature of hope unless we understand it as true and false, and as a consequence both true and false hope must be thinkable if we are to think what it means to be persons. This last step seems to suggest an even more compelling realization, that being a person itself must contain a vivid sense of being a true and a false person, so that in some sense hoping falsely enables us to exist falsely as a person and hoping truly enables us to exist truly as a person. One obvious and in-escapable realization that follows from these suggestions is that as persons able to hope we are finite. In the phenomenon of hope as being both true and false, however, this finitude is not entirely negative: hope suggests the reach of the finite person beyond mere finitude. If hoping can be true what makes it true is the endorsement of our finitude that enables a sense of being more than what we are.

CHAPTER THREE | The Metaxu

The Greek term "metaxu" means "in-between." To anglicize this term gives it a special—one might almost say "technical"—status, suggesting that as linkage it enables what is connected. Plato uses it in the Symposium to suggest that love is 'in between' lacking and having, for as Juliet says: "I long but for the thing I have" when speaking of her status as Romeo's lover and beloved. In the dialogue, however, it becomes clear metaxu can itself be either true or false. Socrates, in order to establish an analogy, first suggests that what is between knowledge and ignorance is true opinion; this however will not sustain the power to illuminate love, hence as metaxu it is false; consequently he substitutes true opinion with philosophical inquiry or dialectic as the proper or true metaxu between ignorance and knowledge, since inquiry links our asking to our learning (actively), but opinion is merely a position (passive) between them. Love is metaxu precisely because we continue to long for and ache to possess that which in some sense we already have, a requiting lover. For the philosopher, however, the point is even greater: as inquirers we are not only suspended between total ignorance and complete knowledge; as lovers of the truth we must in some sense already have—even if in some sense we always already lack—that which we love most ardently: truth. Indeed it is possible to suggest that truth conceived as absolute and total knowledge would not even be truth, in the same sense that beauty must be longed for and ached for in order for it to be beautiful, even if in some sense we 'have' it—Romeo has given himself to her in the promise of marriage, but she still longs; and she yet still longs even after the sating on the marriage bed.

The final discovery of the previous chapter presents us with the suggestion that hope is metaxu. It links, even as it disjoins, our longing with what is longed for; in hope our being finite reaches beyond itself. As hopers, we link our finite existence to the infinite when we pray; but even atheists can realize our radical finitude only in terms of some projected totality or whole which reaches beyond us, however vague that must be. It is not a mere accident that the famous Pauline trilogy consists of virtues that are metaxu: faith is between certain knowledge and total rejection; love is, if Plato is close, between lacking and having; hope links our finitude to that which reaches beyond it. Indeed perhaps virtue itself is metaxu: God does not need virtue, the evil have none, but, for those of us in between it renders us meaningful. However, what now emerges as a suggestion worthy of reflection is a species of existential inversion: it is neither the lover nor the beloved that accounts for love, but love enables lover and beloved; it is not truth that enables inquiry but inquiry enables truth; it is not salvation that enables hope but hope that enables salvation. Here, then is the great irony inherent in all metaxu: the linkage is not derived from what is linked, but the other way around. Only when the linkage enables the linked shall I use "metaxu"; other cases, which are far more frequent, shall simply be called "being between."

In David's psalms we read of being placed half-way between the angels and the beasts. Metaxu in this sense, however, is not simply a position, as we might say New York is half-way between Washington and Boston; it is rather a truth-revealing paradox or even irony that intensifies learning. To become base, as an animal, is not merely an inclination down the measure of metaxu, like driving south from New York puts us closer to Washington and further from Boston. Rather, to become base is possible only because becoming noble matters, and vice versa. Being base, or becoming base, is no longer one possibility among others, it is a disgrace. It is a disgrace not because I start in the middle and then descend; rather it is a disgrace because I am enabled by metaxu to rise as well as fall. The reach for the angels is not a mere possibility, it is a characteristic of my existence; so to descend to bestial existence is a mockery of myself; but this descent and hence self-mockery is also a characteristic of myself. Against all that inclines me away from the angelic within, I cannot rid myself of it; this shunned, unwanted, and pestiferous enablement not only persists in my weary surrender to the base where I would achieve a tranquility by submission, it mocks my self-degrading the more it is abandoned. Those who abandon hope are thus not merely unfortunate, they are wretched. They seek ease and comfort in giving up hope, for they weary of the struggle; but the delusion is grave, because they cannot escape themselves: their torment is greater, not less.

What makes it greater is not that the noble or the angelic is yet a possibility, it is unfortunately still a reality, for it comes with the package of being a person.

The same is true for the northern trip. If a struggler reaches a loftier plane he is still metaxu; the yearning for the base—indeed, even yet being base—is still with him. This persistence of the lower has two opposing consequences: it heightens the sense of accomplishment, yet it also checks our self-esteem: we still know who we are. The point here is not the warning that misfortune may yet topple my climb; nor is it the grim reminder of the transcience of life: remember man that thou are dust. Rather it is the inescapable realization that the base is still within me, not as a mere possibility but as a reality. This both glorifies even as it mutes my rise. If we understand hope as metaxu, the palpable burden of joy is inescapable, as Schiller's ode in Beethoven's music testifies.

It may seem that these reflections somehow mar the glory and soften the censure; but the opposite is true. Only as metaxu is triumph truly glorious and defeat truly ignoble. Being in between enables us to matter at all. It is truth as paradoxic that emerges here demanding our attention: I am enabled of joy by being, as metaxu, both joyful and grim, enabled of greatness by being both petty and magnificent. This finitude is thus a dynamic, not a static finitude. The formal name we can give to our existential, dynamic finitude is hope. Were Paul a philosopher rather than theologian he may have ranked hope above love and faith; love is surely the noblest of the three, since it suggests the achievement of triumph, but hope is the most fundamental, since it enables the triumph.

The philosophical danger yet threatens, however. It is difficult to shake off the persistence that it is the angels and the beasts that are real, and man, as metaxu, is somehow less real, being between them. This persistence is dangerous precisely because it endeavors to understand the human person in terms other than human, beast, and angel, rather than the other way around. We really do not understand beasts and angels as well as we understand ourselves; yet few lines in all literature reveal who we are quite as powerfully as David's psalm. How is this possible? The more I reflect on beasts the more elusive they become: they are not the same as us, in spite of what the radical animal-rights advocates attempt to prosyletize, but they are magnificent, and should not be mistreated. Angels may not exist at all;

but if we entertain them as the scholastics define them they are even more elusive, pure minds without bodies, but still finite: with such a definition they escape any recognition. Two utterly mysterious beings are then used as recognizable opposites between which we, as human persons, are supposed to become intelligible! One may as well explain the word "two" to a child as the square root of twenty-five minus the square root of nine. Why then does David's song work so well? Perhaps one answer might be that hope is of our essence, and what is hoped for and what is hoped against are approachable just because we are not the extremes. This suggestion, however, is merely an exit from the problem rather than a confrontation of it. If hope is existential, dynamic finitude, no mere appeal to what we are not suffices. Knowing I am not a dragon tells me nothing. Yet, knowing I am neither a thief nor a murderer, when conjoined with the realization I am also not a paragon whose radiance sustains others, does seem to tell me something.

Part of the elusiveness inherent in this probing is that only the first part of David's psalm is cited. Being between angels and beasts, he adds, makes it all the more astonishing that God is mindful of us. We are not only stunned by our position between beasts and angels, but that being in this nether would of suspension, we should matter at all; but being so perhaps we matter even more than the dog and the god. Being metaxu failure and success enable us to be who we are, and any input from beyond us would then have some effect. Birds do not need any help to be birds, and gods do not need help to be gods, but we certainly seem to need help to be who we are. Indeed, needing help to be who we are may seem of our essence, which would be rather droll were it not so achingly true. If it is of our essence, it is what is meant by hope. The question now becomes imperative: are these so-called existential inversions valid? Do victory and defeat enable the race, or does the race enable the victor and the defeated? Does truth enable inquiry or inquiry enable truth? Such fundamental asking seems almost arbitrary; in a sense, either perspective is legitimate, for without a victor there is no race and without a race there is no victor. It depends on how we ask. Why race? To win. Who wins? He who races. What is a race? Running that yields winners and losers. How, in this olio of wild askings, can we say there is one way that is fundamental? Are we down to asking about chickens and eggs? The contempt that lurks behind this last question is salvatory, for in asking it we uncover that how and what we ask does indeed matter. Merely because various ways of asking are possible does not entail they are equally meaningful. To toss out the various ways of asking may seem to trivialize the inquiry—indeed if we merely strew the confetti of different colored askings and leave them floating without further reflection, abandoning them with a superior smirk because we have rendered them silly, we have indeed trivialized. What we trivialize, however, is not the questioning but ourselves. These questions are not without meaningful responses.

Hope is metaxu: it is being in the middle. In the middle of what? We say: we are suspended between beast and angel. We understand this even if we seriously doubt there are angels, and even if we are unsure what to make of beasts. There is, in us, both the angelic and the bestial. When Lincoln urges us to attend to the better angels of our nature we realize the profundity of his appeal even if we deny there are real angels. We have a privileged access to our own nature as beyond or beneath ourselves. That we are somehow in between them is clearer and more revealing than what constitutes nobility, what is beyond—and what is beneath, baseness. Since we are between them, to be able to be an angel or a dog must be rooted in this suspension. The unshunnable middle is therefore fundamental, and being so it enables both baseness and nobility. In exactly the same way that fear is the basis of both cowardice and courage, and racing the basis of victory and defeat, our being between, as hope, enables our approach to the gods. But is hope also that which enables our approach to the dogs? Surely that is not hope but despair.

Perhaps then, it is misleading to suggest that hope is existential suspension; rather it is suspension inclined toward nobility. This, however, is deeply troubling, for then it becomes necessary to account for our suspension by what is linked rather than the linkage, and we are forced back to a dualism. Is not a race equally determined by winner and loser? No. We strive to win, not to lose. In a race we run in order to win, thus winning grounds the race. Granted there must be a loser, but losing is not why we race. The loser is a failed racer, not a non-racer, but racing itself is thinkable in terms of its ground: why we race—to win. Hope, by analogy, is not a mere co-possibility with despair; rather it is more fundamental since it provides the reason for being in the suspension. As metaxu, hope enables both angels and dogs, but not equally, for hope is positive since its goal or end is to reach beyond as toward the angel. Yet, even were the angelic reached it would still be an angel capable of becoming a dog and were we to fall to the level of a dog it would be a dog yet able to be an angel.

With this discovery, however, there is a danger. Hope is not the same as freedom or responsibility—indeed in some sense hope is opposed to responsibility, for my free acts are due to my agency, whereas hope reaches beyond myself. A critic of the above paragraphs may legitimately point out that suspension between baseness or beasts and nobility or angels simply is freedom; I am responsible for my baseness and nobility: hope has nothing to do with it. The point of such criticism is valid, but misdirected. The usage of the terms "nobility" and "baseness" in the above description is not moral but existential: "noble" means reaching beyond our humanity, "base" means falling below it. Nevertheless, the criticism is mentioned here because it enables a deeper reflection. In what way does the existential metaxu of hope connect with the moral metaxu of freedom? Am I free to hope or despair? Is hoping entirely unlinked to morally free acts? To raise the question of the metaxu between hope and moral freedom requires a fresh origin.

Who and what we are as persons seems to be rendered thinkable only by making a fundamental distinction. On the one hand there are acts that I perform that seem to be the result of my willing them, thereby constituting a part of my existence over which I have control. I seem to be responsible for my willful acts, and am held responsible by myself and others, so that I am censured for immoral acts and praised for good acts. On the other hand, I seem to be entirely lacking in any control whatsoever in many things that happen to me or account for who I am. I did not choose my birth nor my native language; I have no say over the weather or the acts of most other people. Yet, as my story unfolds there seems to be some species of coherence about the passages of my temporal becoming, at least to the point that I can talk about the ungoverned dimensions of my existence as shaping who I am. What is controlled by me is often called the product of my willing; what is not controlled but still affects me is often called my fate or destiny. As long as we do not reify these influences into substances there is no danger in the simple acceptance of the fact that much, perhaps even most, of what is meaningful in my life is beyond my willful control. We may say we are blessed or cursed, lucky or unlucky, smiled at or frowned at by fortune, victims of cruel coincidence or favored by fortuitous circumstance. However we refer to it, we see it as opposed to what is the product of my willful planning. For the sake of convenience we may designate what is un-controlled and unplanned about my story as fate, and designate what is controlled as freedom. By this distinction no claim about the metaphysical status of either is intended; the two terms refer simply to the two different ways we seem to think about what shapes our historical—that is, tempo-ral—existence. With this distinction we now can ask: does hope belong to fate or to freedom?

It may seem at first that hope is entirely a matter of fate. If I hope my friend's blood test turns out benign it must be because I can do nothing about making it benign. I should not say I hope to keep my promise, since keeping it is a matter of will; I might say I hope to be able to keep my promise, for that seems to concern whether the future conditions, over which I have no control, will not impede me from doing what I ought, and indeed will, to do. Even if I give religious form to my hope by praying, I am still admitting I do not entirely control the matter. Hope therefore does not require the thinker to establish a metaphysical basis for arbitrariness, for whether I conceive the future to be the workings of a willful God or the sheer serendipity of fortune or even a combination of the two is irrel-evant to the fact that what I hope is not entirely up to me, and thus is a matter of fate, not freedom.

This first impression, however, may not suffice. It seems clear we can and do will to hope, for if we could not it would make no sense to urge someone to keep on hoping when difficulties arise. Further, the possibility that hope may take the form of prayer is not as idle as it may seem, for if there is a personal deity, we as agents decide to pray or not, and what we pray for is a willful intervention of a free superior agency controlling what will happen. Even from an atheistic perspective, hoping seems to be a per-sonal resistance to the sheer indifference of rank arbitrariness or the wanton distribution of coincidence. To hope seems at the very least to adopt an at-titude of concern for what might happen, therefore it is opposed to the at-titude of indifference. The world itself may be indifferent, but to hope is to reject this indifference as the only significant way to think about the world. If the world is truly indifferent in the complexity of coincidence, is not hope, for a metaphysical naturalist, entirely irrational? The naturalist may well respond by pointing out that a species that hopes, in the course of evolution, is a more successful species than one that does not; that hoping is a psychological boost necessary to get through bad times, and a species that avails itself of such boosts weathers the evolutionary erosion better than a similar species that does not. Even with this rejoinder, however, hope emerges as a characteristic of the free, rather than the fated modalities of existence, for it freely adopts an attitude toward an indifferent world that itself is not indifferent.

To the earlier suggestion that hope is dynamic finitude can now be added a more refined suggestion concerning hope as metaxu: what hope links is our being fated with our being free. It seems a fundamental necessity to disjoin fate from freedom; yet it is also an existential imperative to conjoin them, for I am not two persons—one fated, the other free—but one person both fated and free. This conjunction cannot merely be asserted, it must be accounted, and the suggestion now reaches its critical mass: hope, as dynamic or existential finitude, alone can conjoin our being free and being fated. Since we obviously are both fated and free, and since these two ways of existing seem oppositional in some sense, it is needful to understand ourselves as being able to be both. This "being able to be both" is now revealed as the fundamental modality of hope. Reflection on this discovery is now demanded by the inquiry.

Suppose I hope a friend receives my urgent message. To some extent, since I sent the message, I am its agent: it is a product of my will. The mechanics of the message itself, however, are beyond my control. Whether the e-mail, voice-mail or written note is read, picked up, or delivered at all is beyond my power. To say I hope he receives it, however, is not merely to recognize that I sent the message and do not control its being received. For, having sent it, I continue, as willful, to care about the success of its delivery and reception. It is not in my control that it be received, but it is in my control to care that it be received. This care takes the form of trust in the machinery of delivery and reception, including the willingness of my friend to read a message that comes from me. Is this hoping merely a psychological desire? Or is it rather the linkage between what I control and what I cannot control? Only if my hope takes the form of prayer can I maintain that the outcome may be influenced though not determined, by my free agency. But even if I do not pray but only hope, the act of hoping itself is within my control to some extent; more importantly, adopting the willful attitude of hoping towards what might be an entirely indifferent world is not the same as adopting an attitude of indifference that would correspond to the indifference of the world. My being hopeful therefore reaches into the unmanageable world as if part of the indifferent can be made different. I need not at all believe my hoping is a cause that might actually alter the world, as prayer might; but such hoping can and often does profoundly alter me. At the very least it alters me by revealing the curious status of being between as metaxu. I am not only fated and free, but free as fated and fated as free. Hope, therefore, cannot be a mere wish about the future—though it may also be that—it is rather an uncovering of one of the most fundamental ironies of our existence: our finitude is dynamic.

Hope as metaxu can be but slenderly grasped as long as the referent is to an actual case of one person hoping for a desirable outcome, for the tendency in such cases is to see it merely as desire. There is no reason to prohibit the use of the term 'hope' in such cases; the prohibition is in the restriction of the usage only to such cases. In the opening chapter various literary usages were noted that far exceed the common usage; two of which now stand out. The first is the usage that sees hope as a species of prayer, the second is the usage by Kant that sees hope as a species of reason. In both of these remarkable cases, hope as metaxu is palpable. In prayer hope links the human as person to the divine as person; in reason, hope links the coherence of moral thinking with the seeming incoherence of actual injustice in the world provided by experience. Each of these deserves separate analyses on their own, but for the moment it is enough to trace briefly the outline of hope as metaxu in each.

If we provisionally assume that prayer is not mere superstition, we must recognize the enormity of what is implied. A finite being, whose resources as finite are fairly grim if not outright depressing, somehow is enabled to supplicate as a finite person to a transfinite if not an infinite person—if an infinite person is not a contradiction in terms. Such supplication cannot be guaranteed, yet neither can it be rendered entirely feckless. The mind is so staggered by the enormity of the problems inherent with a divine listener that these issues dominate our discourse. Why are some prayers answered and others not? How can God be good if he allows evil? How are we to consider the possibilities of intervention in a world governed

by natural laws? These mighty and legitimate questions so overwhelm that
the problems concerning the finite supplicant—the one who prays—are almost buried. Yet these problems are closer to us and are no less profound.
Who am I that I should be listened to? What does it mean that some of my
prayers are left unanswered? Unanswered, am I less or more worthy? How
can I be free if another's prayers about me are answered? What does it mean
if I am answered at all? These questions about the supplicant all presuppose
an underlying, fundamental one: is prayer enabled by hope?

   To find ourselves already in the world, yet able in some restricted sense
to act in this world in such a way as to be held responsible, requires a certain
bifurcation in how we think about ourselves: I am a pawn of forces beyond
myself, yet an agent that consciously manipulates parts of the world for my
own purpose. When my consciously generated projects are inserted as
causes into world, they intrude into an already busy complex of other forces,
not all of which can continue as they were prior to my intervention. To reflect upon this reality—that my projects enter into the stream of countering
forces—reveals my status as object and subject, mover and moved, fated
and free. Insofar as my project matters to me, I must care about its success
both as generated by me and as independent of my influence. To pray is to
locate the uncontrollable dimension of my caring into another realm of persons, so that not only is the origin of my project rooted in a person (myself
as willing agent), but the success and subsequent continuation of the project
is also rooted in a person, a person who not only may heed my entreaty but
also is enabled to influence the project once it has left the safe anchorage
of my will. In this way, the project becomes no longer merely my project,
but also, because I matter to the person of a higher power, it now becomes
his project as well. Thus, in supplicant praying I unite my project with my
fate in such a way that my fate is no longer a mere abyss of uncertainty and
interlocking possibilities, but a project of another person, powerful enough
to enable the project to be realized or at least supported by means of his
own projecting. If hope is the connection and enabler of both realms—
what I influence and what I do not—prayer is nothing else but hope linked
to a personal power beyond my reach and ken. In this way the existential
reality of being both pawn and projector lies as the fundamental basis which
enables prayer at all. As thinker, therefore, what is immediate in its availability to me is my own existential status as free and fated, projector and

pawn; what is mediate—because it lies beyond me—is the metaphysical as-sertion of a supernatural realm peopled by at least one divine person. Hope thus is the existential basis of prayer; but it is the basis only as metaxu—being between fate and freedom by being both.

It is not only prayer, however, but reason itself that is enabled by our being in dynamic suspension between our fate and our freedom. Being able to think about the world as a possible threat to my projects—what might be called the indifference of the actual within the world—and being able to think about myself as free and hence morally significant, are not merely two different ways of thinking, they are also two different ways of existing based upon the two different ways of thinking. To think of myself as mo-rally significant—and hence to be morally significant—I must care about at least two fundamental realms in which I dwell: the realm revealed en-tirely by my own realization of what I ought to do—my duty, and the realm revealed by experience, particularly my experience of the acts and fates of others. This second realm provides me with the ineluctable realization that the acts and fates of others are seemingly impervious to what I know about myself as morally significant: the realm of experience with others shows me there is no—or very little—justice, by which virtue is meant that the good are rewarded and the bad are punished. The facts show me that the wicked on the whole succeed and the upright fail. As Plato points out in the second book of the Republic, most of us, given the ring of Gyges, would take immoral advantage of it, revealing the factual principle: it is better merely to appear just but to be truly selfish, disregarding others—to be un-just. Thus, my cognitive resources reveal a dilemma if not an inconsistency: the way the world is does not correspond to the way it ought to be.

Several philosophical attempts have been made to accommodate this non-correspondence. We may follow certain indifferentists, particularly those that have eastern or fatalist origins, and admit this fact but refuse to be moved by it. An impressive variant of this view is the stoic doctrine that virtue is its own reward: it is better to be cruelly imprisoned for being good than to be free and opportunistically pleasured for being bad. There is something noble about this indifference, but it is curiously ignoble as well since among the virtues is justice, and I ought to care about the injustice done to others if not myself; but it is precisely the injustice done to others that I cannot rectify. Kant sees in this non-correspondence an unacceptable clash or disharmony among the faculties of cognition. It is not merely that the unjust are rewarded and the just tormented, it is rather that my own consciousness is in rebellion against itself because of this realization. As rational we cannot abide internal inconsistency, and so, as rational, I am compelled to postulate whatever would re-establish the correspondence. For Kant it is meaningful to talk about reason as a source of postulates: to be able to reason includes being able to postulate reasonably. What is postulated—though never known or proven—is God and an afterlife. Such postulation not only brings about justice (eventually) but, apparently more importantly for Kant, it provides the internal harmony among the faculties. Kant identifies this reason-based postulation as rational hope, making hope a necessary part of reasoning itself. We are less rational if we do not hope.

Those who are chary of any theological claim may scorn this seeming back-door approach, as if we sneak God into our philosophical vocabulary on the thin and messy activity of postulating wantonly. What such scorn overlooks, however, is that what Kant postulates—God and an afterlife—is less important than that we rationally postulate at all. In any other case, were our faculties to conflict, the appeal to postulation would seem entirely defensible. Seeing the stick appear bent when immersed in water conflicts with our fingers feeling this same stick as straight; we then must postulate that either our eyes or our fingers are misleading us, for the one thing we do not allow is the contradiction that would ensue if both faculties, touch and sight, are believed. Inconsistency among the faculties requires postulation, even if only provisionally; it is the way our consciousness works. Kant points out we must postulate something that will accommodate both faculties; and he labels this need for postulation, hope. Hope is therefore a necessary ingredient in our reasoning, particularly in our self-reflective reasoning in which some species of harmony must exist between our moral reasoning and our reasoning about justice. To say this postulation is required by and constitutes a part of our reasoning is to say there is authority in hoping—the authority provided by reason itself. If this is so, hope cannot be a mere emotion since such emotions have no authority in themselves at all.

If Kant is formally correct, we must be able to postulate, and it is this ability that links our faculties—hope. Hope is, as that which enables us to postulate, a function of reason, and is necessarily metaxu: that is—it is a link that enables the faculties to belong to one consciousness. We must think of rational hope as an authoritative metaxu: a reason-based linkage between what we ought to do and what we care about as being just. Reason as a faculty is not merely a disconnected amagalm of various ways of being reasonable: doing science, doing math, doing moral reflection; rather it is a connected and hence coherent authority by which these various ways are interconnected. Hope provides the connection, hence hope is a species of reasoning; non-hope is therefore irrational.

The significance of the analysis of hope as metaxu must be pushed. Common reflection may see hope as a mere psychological connection between my present state of desiring what I lack and my projection into a future in which that desire will be fulfilled. Now, however, the suggestion has emerged that what seems a mere connection is a genuine metaxu: an enabling power that synthesizes fundamental ways of thinking and being. In supplicant prayer, hope enables the union of the human and divine; as a species of reasoning it provides for a synthesis or harmony of our faculties. In both cases the nature of the metaxu avails the regions brought together: it is only by hope that we learn what it means to be suspended between God and man; it is only by hope that reasoning is enabled to be itself reasonable. If the status of hope as an existential metaxu is to be seen more than a mere formal requirement, however, the phenomenon itself now must be examined in a light made brighter by these reflections.

CHAPTER FOUR | The Word

Hope is a word. To say this is not to suggest it is a mere word, as we might say of a leprechaun. It is, however, important to spot hope as a word, for words are used in language, and like all words, their use by the great and the profound becomes a resource for inquirers into truth. In seeking to understand words, everyday usage does not have hegemony; a great poet or orator or a profound thinker can welcome back the power of a word exiled by banal prose. To say hope, as a word, is found in language is to realize it participates in the event or happening of discourse, especially that species of discourse that manifests itself self-consciously in terms of the forms that make language work as language and not merely as verbal reference or labeling. These forms include what are known as figures of speech. To understand hope we must, then, reflect how it works as a word, that is, how it operates within figures, as well as locution, syntax, and even style. A few selections may afford some meaty insights.

Having been chided by the duke for his rude and threatening entrance, Orlando is moved to entreat pardon:

> Speak you so gently? Pardon me, I pray you:
> I thought that all things had been savage here;
> And therefore put I on the countenance
> Of stern commandment. But whate'er you are
> That in this desert inaccessible,
> Under the shade of melancholy boughs,
> Lose and neglect the creeping hours of time;
> If ever you have look'd on better days,
> If ever been where bells have knoll'd to church,
> If ever sat at any good man's feast,
> If ever from your eyelids wip'd a tear,
> And know what 'tis to pity and be pitied,

Let gentleness my strong enforcement be:
In the which hope I blush, and hide my sword.
                                        (*As You Like It*, II, 7)

The entire passage is necessary for us to appreciate this singular use of
"hope" in the last line. How are we to understand the phrase "in the which
hope"? Does Orlando sheath his sword because he hopes the duke and his
men have looked on better days? Or is his sheathing itself an act of hope,
suggesting hope is akin to trust? Perhaps here the single term "hope" refers
to the prior six lines that describe a world of gentility so enchanting it tells
us why and for what we hope at all. Or is hope merely that which provokes
Orlando to blush? Perhaps hope here simply reflects its hypothetical essence, reinforcing the word "if" that begins each of lines 8 through 11? In
what sense does the word "hope" counter his expectation of savagery in the
second line? What is Orlando hoping for? Perhaps in this passage it is improper to identify what is hoped, for it may be that the word here points
not to any expectation but to a realization: these men, he realizes, are gentle.
Yet, there is much that is tenuous in the passage—all those "ifs" have their
effect—suggesting that perhaps hope here is not so much akin to trust as
it is to courage; Orlando is willing to take the risk; he is still the bold young
man who enters an uncertain stage with sword drawn: he hopes as courageous. There is, of course, a plainer reading: perhaps the poet uses the word
"hope" simply as a synonym for "case": "in which case I hide my sword."
Even if we accept this, however, we still want to know what is different in
using hope rather than case. That we can use hope in lieu of case is itself
an exciting discovery, for with this diction the former term can refer to a
general set of circumstance that favors, and hence not merely to the psychological feeling of the personal, singular one who hopes.

This listing of possible meanings serves as an opening wedge to how
the term "hope" functions in the broader language of the art-form. It is
possible that all of these suggestions are contained in this particular poetic
usage, and such reflection may enrich our appreciation of the literary passage. No mere listing, however, is enough; indeed not all suggestions in
any list are equally worthy; some may be distracting or even unacceptable.
It may be helpful to explore another possible reading that may stretch a
bit, but which nevertheless isolates an aspect of Orlando's speech not to be

overlooked. In other plays by Shakespeare, especially Antony and Cleopatra, the term "sword" is used as a metaphor for the phallus, and such usage may seem to apply here because of the words "blush" and "hide." Furthermore, if the overall imagery of the passage is the contrast between gentility and savagery, the suggestion of hiding one's genitals in shame may reinforce the notion that Orlando's entrance was uncivil, as if he had intruded on the scene in naked barbarity. It may be an indulgence, however, to read such venereal meaning into an otherwise chaste passage, but this suggestion directs our attention to the words "hide" and "blush." We blush at what shames; shame drives us to cover ourselves or hide. "in the which hope I blush and hide…" must now be read compactly, mingling each term like subtle seasonings in a sauce. It is the hope itself that shames; "the which hope" means: this particular species of hoping—the species that makes us hide. How does hope provoke the blush, and hence the hiding? It is now no longer possible to restrict our reading to the passage; the play itself intrudes, a play that echoes hope in its very name: As you like it.

The ousted duke is introduced to us, the audience, with his first words assuring us how "sweet are the uses of adversity." Even his own followers are moved to admire his courage and sweetness in the face of "the stubbornness of fortune." This nobility is not restricted to the duke; it sauces the entire feast of the play, from Adam and Orlando to Silvius and Rosalind. The forest of Auden is a concretization of hope—not just any hope, but hope based on nobility, sweetness and courage. The noble hope by which the duke finds sweetness in adversity and force in gentleness, shames the naked, savage, and brutal brandish of a sword. When Orlando hides his weapon it is in the face of this noble hope that reveals itself as, and not merely in, the forest of Auden. It is the court, from which the duke, Rosalind, and Orlando have been banished, that is raw, uncivil, and savage; it is the court with all its seeming civility, that mocks hope. In this passage, therefore, the word "hope" is not futuristic, nor is it a species of desire, it is a way of being; a confrontation of adversity as sweetness; a blush at one's incivility thereby showing, in the shame, the deeply civil; it is something we are, not something we merely aspire to become. "In the which hope" now means: "in the face of this nobility," to which Orlando properly belongs. We do not blush at guilt; Orlando justifies drawing his sword as a legitimate act based on fear and ignorance. What makes him blush is thus not the immorality of the act, but the shame of standing rudely before men who are not rude. He is unexpectedly denuded by his unchaste sword, hanging there in his youthful hand. He does not sheath it at the onset of his speech, but at its end; so that throughout his radiant plea for civility and grace, the weapon grows more and more unseemly, mocking his own vulnerability. He prefaces the sheathing with the intonation of what his presence before the nobles means: in the which hope. He hides his shameful nakedness by the assurance of his own worth; the phrase "in the which hope" simply verbalizes that assurance—it is the assurance. Hope is that way of being that enables his self-discovery through shame; his own nobility now companions the duke's men. Hope as a way of being is the sheathing of a naked sword.

Reinforcement for this reading of Orlando's use of the term "hope" is adumbrated by the magnificent opening speech of the duke. Even ordinary, everyday understanding of hope includes finding sweetness in the uses of adversity. We identify one as hopeful who does not whimper in self-pity at life's disappointment but boldly confronts them, trusting that not mere good experiences but all of human experience, including the bad, can be in service of our character and our learning. The audience's response to the duke's noble civility itself may be called hope, for by confronting and absorbing the scene we are led to rely upon the ultimate triumph of what is worthy in us over the cowardly feelings of hopelessness in the face of setback and disappointment. This is an appeal to hope even in its vernacular usage; we are assured by this that Shakespeare's use of the term "hope" is not extravagant but universal.

Nevertheless, the duke's speech offers far more than a mere boost to our own feelings of hope, so a closer look at the passage may be in order:

Here feel we but the penalty of Adam,
The season's difference: as the icy fang
And churlish chiding of the winter's wind,
Which when it bites and blows upon my body,
Even till I shrink with cold, I smile and say,
This is no flattery: these are counselors
That feelingly persuade me what I am.
Sweet are the uses of adversity;

> Which, like the toad, ugly and venomous,
> Wears yet a precious jewel in his head;
> And this our life, exempt from public haunt,
> Finds tongues in trees, books in the running brooks,
> Sermons in stones, and good in everything.
> I would not change it.

It would be churlish to deny this is a passage about hope. Yet, hope now becomes a deeper, worthier commodity of spirit. The bites and blows of winter are "counselors that feelingly persuade me what I am." Being persuaded what we are is existential truth. The court is a deceit; the forest a place of self-discovery. But truth is the jewel in the head of the toad; it is the supreme lure of philosophy itself. We thus link the inquiry into hope with the hope of inquiry, truth. This coupling is so remarkable it deserves a moment's reflection.

The surface reading seems clear: the flattery of the court is deceit: the sycophancy, the protected security, the pomp and falseness of will, easily distract us from truth, especially and above all from truth as self-discovery. This contrasts with the icy fangs of the forest's winter reminding us that beneath the glitter and baubles of the court we are still men; we are closer to the earth and its honest appraisal of our limits and finitude. What disturbs in this surface reading, however, is the suggestion that if the forest were to represent a total stripping away of civil refinement, the result would be as Orlando feared: we would return to savagery. Reduced to the level of sheer survival, we become base. Is there, then, not a naive, pastoral romanticism in the duke's praise of Arden? Only displaced courtiers wax nostalgic about the return to nature. This is the danger—a very real, anti-philosophical danger—in the surface reading, requiring a more cautious learning. There are a few obvious cleats on the wharf of the text to which we can attach our cables against this drift. The duke is not savage; indeed neither are those born in Arden. Orlando and the men around the duke are not native to Auden; they are well born and well bred, so that as ex-courtiers they still bear with them the refinement of education. (The play opens, we remind ourselves, with Orlando's complaint he has not been offered the education he deserves.) Certainly the language of the exiles is noble. What then does the duke mean when he identifies the adversities of Arden as counselors that feelingly persuade him who he is? His great, final line, "and good in everything" does not say there is only good in everything; the gift of truth as self-discovery—which now may be called hope—includes our spotting the ills without eclipsing our worth. We shun the surface reading of naive romanticism in part because we recognize it is not anyone and everyone in Arden who learn about themselves, but only those already enabled in their character, a list that includes some born in Arden. With the tugging of the surface romantic drift resisted by these solid cleats in the text, the true reading emerges more freely and more profoundly: hope is hope because of truth, not because of illusion. The duke is not a naive romantic, for he learns from the pains of his exile; even his most rewarding lesson, that the boy Ganymede is his beloved daughter Rosalind, is learned by her deceit that revealed: she first had to disguise herself in order to reveal herself. Philosophical truth must endure the pangs of uncertain inquiry which may deviate, but taking these false paths and retreating back on them make them true paths; the overall journey of truth is hope. This coupling of hope to philosophical inquiry is suggested by the duke's assertion that winter's fangs rend open the truth of his existence—it is more than that, but that suffices; indeed it is a bounty the expenditure of which must provisionally be delayed. It is enough now to see the glitter.

In one of the most radiant of lyric poems written in English, "Lullaby," the poet W. H. Auden tells us:

> Soul and Body have no bounds:
> To lovers as they lie upon
> Her tolerant enchanted slope
> In their ordinary swoon,
> Grave the vision Venus sends
> Or supernatural sympathy,
> Universal love and hope;
> While an abstract insight wake
> Among the glaciers and the rocks
> The hermit's carnal ecstasy.

Venus, the love goddess, sends us a vision of universal love and hope. What hope means in this line requires the whole stanza; but the immediate question is palpable: how can hope be universal? The conjunction suggests it is like universal love; but how can love be universal? Only a grim pedant would reduce this figure to the abstract universality of all nouns, enabling us to say the dog has a sensitive nose, meaning all dogs have good noses. What, then, is meant by universal hope? And why is it coupled with love?

Part of the power of this poem is its treasure in the unlikely. This is a one-night stand, an opportunistic coupling ignited by mere lust that unexpectedly rages into a fierce if brief inferno of erotic ecstasy. In this furnace glows the light and heat of true love, however fleeting; and being ephemeral, all the more stunning in its discovery. It is a dangerous piece, seeming to endorse promiscuity; it is also a near-bawdy sentiment, suggesting wanton pleasures can be justified as possible origins of universal redemption. Yet, it is a true piece, all the more perilous because it is true. What gives it an almost vertiginous risk is what it shows us about hope as the third in the list of three: supernatural sympathy, universal love, and—but are we sure the adjective applies to the final noun? The poet clearly says that love is universal; but the rules of syntax allow us to apply universality either to love only or to both love and hope. Still, it seems the natural reading to let the adjective modify both nouns. The hope endangers in any event. The aliens to those on Venus' slope, and hence the antagonists to this dangerous message are the puritans; or perhaps more dangerous still, the moralists. Is it merely puritanic to insist that "every dreaded cost shall be paid," or is it morality that demands payment? Is the hope found in Venus, immoral? If it is puritanic to say so, we can dismiss it easily; but if it is truly immoral we are in deep peril indeed. The lover-poet gives us too many hints: human, guilty, faithless—he finds the mortal world enough. These are the tocsins of an ethical bell, not the false alarums of a pedant or puritan. Are we really to find hope, universal or singular, in what ought not to be?

Perhaps that is what hope is: the lure of beauty entreating the sinner. Auden has not abandoned theism; he still speaks of supernatural sympathy; his orthography is rich in theological diction. Even if we bracket or foreclose the moral dubiety, there is yet the anguish entailed in the passage. The poet tells us that the lovers on Venus' slope are in their ordinary swoon. Ordinary! That is a term that clamors against all that poets and philosophers whisper; the ordinary are dull, common, base; they are Nietzsche's last men and Shakespeare's rabble and Heidegger's inauthentic selves; they are even Auden's own depiction in the poem "Unknown Citizen." How are we to learn from the ordinary? The orthography widens, however: it is the ordinary to whom Venus sends the grave vision. In true love the ordinary, who may be merely rutting in the back seat, becomes extraordinary, even if only for a one-night stand—or perhaps we should say the one-night lie. This grave vision of universality in love and hope sent to the ordinary contrasts with the vision sent to the extraordinary: for the already grave hermit is sparked with the ungrave fire of carnal ecstasy.

Both grave hermit and ordinary lover are thus lifted by eros—that species of love that weaves the warp of lust to the woof of aching devotion, and hence must always startle—but this rise is scowled by those whom Auden calls the pedants. It is the puritanic pedant who chides the lovers, both grave and ordinary; but this chiding is not the spiritual censure of those who ardently care for chastity as a virtue; for if we listen to their warning it is far more base than that. The pedants worry not about the loss of virtue but the loss of cash: "every farthing must be paid." Your indiscretions will have dire and expensive consequences: unwanted pregnancies, bad feelings, venereal diseases, embarrassing discovery—these are the pedantic, boring cries that would quench the fires of lust and with them, those of eros as well. Yet, though the poet calls these alarmists both boring and pedantic, they still cry what is true. Their being true simply does not eclipse what the lover may learn in the precious, stolen hours of a love-night: universal hope.

If hope is to be universal it cannot be a mere specific wish; being universal it must lie fundamentally in the very essence of the human soul. Even if we realize this, it is not yet clear why the universal should number hope among its children. We must ask what hope does such that in doing it its universality becomes manifest. Auden's poem makes it very clear: hope finds in the ordinary what is extraordinary; hope makes an incision into the singular to lay open the universal; hope turns a saucy tumble in the back seat of a car into a stunned submission of love's power. It is not lust alone that does this, but lust coupled with hope that spawns true, even if fleeting, love. The ascetic hermit may seek to escape the bondage of his sinews, but universal hope awakes even in him the unexpected carnal ecstasy. Why is this discovery of the rare in the prolix of the common identified as hope? Why not read the passage as spotting love, rather than hope, as the origin of these things? Precisely because we distinguish the merely carnal from the erotic and the erotic from devotional fidelity, it cannot be love alone that links itself to non-loving lust: the emergence of the former from the latter is neither inevitable nor inherent in the nature of either lust or love. Not all who lust, love; not all who love do so in erotic ecstasy. Love by itself does not, then, explain the emergence from the ordinary lovers on Venus' slope to the extraordinary. Love must be coupled with hope to enable this mutation from fire to fireworks that stun the night's sky. It is hope, therefore, as a universal gift to those lying on Venus' slope, that ascends and bursts in a spray of light.

What does Auden's ranking hope with supernatural sympathy and universal love tell us about what hope means? The metaphor is simple and telling: hope enables the ordinary swoon to become extraordinary; hope also allows the purely spiritual love of the hermit to be snarled with the ligatures of carnal passion. Is this really so surprising? The hope is that our visceral stirrings may raise us to genuine love—or rather: that the carnal may transform us to lovers. Less obviously, but still defensibly, the hermit may in his purist grasp of the abstract, be stirred by fire. Universality can mean various things; it means the entire class: all fires are hot; it means inherent in the essence: the patriot, in loving his homeland is willing to sacrifice for it; it means law-like: events must have causes, criminals ought to be punished; it means paradigm: Romeo shows us what it means to be a lover; it also means ideal in the sense of reasoning toward perfection, as Plato does in the Republic. If hope is universal, and, when linked with love, it reveals the extraordinary in the ordinary, then Auden's poem curiously coincides with Kant's analysis, that hope universalizes concretely by reuniting body with soul, mind with spirit, flesh with heart, reason with feeling—that is, it establishes a harmony of the faculties.

Nevertheless there yet seems something of license in this generous reading. Even if we admit it is hope and not mere love that enables the universal in the existentially concrete, it has not been shown that hope alone does this. Indeed hope as hope, rather than hope linked with love in Auden's poem or hope linked to nobility in Shakespeare's passage, seems an urchin on the streets of discourse. The word seems to take on glorious dimensions when linked to other glories, but by itself it seems curiously inept. Is hope a chameleon or a catalyst, or perhaps even a parasite? Its worth and meaning seems to rely on its power to enhance that to which it is attached. This need not be seen as an entire indictment, for if hope needs something else to make it hope it is then not entirely dissimilar to a midwife, not bearing children herself but assisting in the birth. It is Plato in the Theaetetus who describes philosophy as midwifery—no cheap company in this! That hope may be a midwife to love, to nobility, even to truth, may not be, then, a defect. The title and first sentence of this chapter now offers an entrance-ramp to the highway of further discovery. Are words themselves midwives? Is the word "love" a midwife to loving? It can be. At times, the most erotic moment in the entire wooing of the beloved is when the hesitant, green youth confesses and thus denudes his soul by saying "I am in love with you." Such words may not merely describe an already existing state, they may establish it, bring it to full life, as the midwife pulls the unborn into infancy. These dire but radiant words may seem to erupt unbidden from some inner volcanic violence, humbling the speaker as it elevates. Are these words the midwife to the thought? to the action? to the love itself? If so, and if philosophy is midwifery to truth, we now must ask if hope is a midwife, and if so, to what?

In reference to language as calling, from *What is Called Thinking*, Martin Heidegger uses the following as an embodiment of "heien"—to call: "Eine Stimme heit uns hoffen. Sie winkt uns das Hoffen zu, ldt dazu ein, befiehlt uns der Hoffnung an, verweist in sie." (151) This is translated by Wieck and Gray in the following way: "A voice calls us to hope. It beckons us to hope, invites us, commands us, directs us to hope." (123) It is not a mere accident that Heidegger should select hope as an example of that which is called or called forth, for hope itself is a species of calling forth, as midwifery brings forth the child and philosophical midwifery calls forth the truth, and hope calls forth hope. The calling forth becomes almost indistinguishable from that which is called forth. If words, as concretized callings, are midwives to truth, they are, in their profoundest usage, a species of truth.

We say "the day is darkening"; we then say the sentence refers to the fact that the day darkens. The words serve as midwives to the truth of the sentence, meaning that when put into words there is a representation in our consciousness that corresponds to what is outside our consciousness; the words extract, as a midwife extracts a babe, a truth from the mere tacit world, uniting world and consciousness. Without the words there would be no truth, but the origin of the truth is still the world; it is the mother who establishes the reality, the midwife who brings it to consciousness; so truth is the link between mind and world. This seems innocent enough. However, when Catholics call the head of their church "pope," papam—father—or subjects call their king "sire"—father—or when we call sequoias "redwoods" or pipe fittings male or female, we call forth an image that helps us understand. In such cases the words seem closer to what they name; when we tremblingly confess to ourselves and our beloved that we have fallen in love, the verbal confession seems more than a mere midwife; they reveal, arouse, stun, as words. When we hereby solemnly swear, the verbal act becomes a performative act. If these words are midwives they seem so in an almost literal sense; they bring forth the truth, they establish the present commitment and thereby change the future. If hope is a midwife as words and philosophical inquiry are midwives, then the fact that hope as hope emerges most clearly when linked to companion words like love and truth is not unexpected. It may further be noted that this suggestion that hope is akin to midwifery seems to gain support from the earlier analysis of it as metaxu. It is as it links. What it links has been variously called: the extraordinary from out of the ordinary, the soul to the body, the moral with the just, the finite in face of the infinite.

In all these uses hope seems an untitled son; the duke to the prince, outranked by primogeniture. If we overlook his presence it is because of the greater radiance of the heir apparent: the second in Paul's triad, but the third in Auden's and Kant's lists. If the first son gets the title, the second, waiting, becomes a warrior; but the third, like Orlando, is too well born to work as ordinary laborer, but too impoverished and outranked to find any noble position; so, either like Richard III he plots to kill his elder brothers, or, more decently, he is quietly shuffled off to a monastery or parsonage, the last, poor, refuge; he must bask, if he basks at all, in vicarage. Midwife indeed—quickly forgotten after the joy of the childbirth, paid off cheaply and sent home. It is the mother and the child who matter. Hope, like philosophy and midwifery and third-born sons, may have royal blood but no royal authority. Gold and frankincense we understand, but what is myrrh? Father and Son we grasp, but what is the Holy Spirit? Male and female, yes; but what then? Eunuch? Hermaphrodite? Freak?

We reflect on the word hope as it is used in great literature; that is the theme of this chapter. Two things are noted: hope rarely stands alone; we speak of pure love or even pure faith, but rarely of pure hope. We also note that when we list things, hope is usually last, as if thrown in as an afterthought. Granted that the company it keeps is lofty indeed, it seems only that: company to the great, perhaps not great itself; or if great, it is great because of its companions. Yet the third position of these literary lists is not always so pale. Medieval thinkers list the three transcendentals as the true, the good, and the beautiful. As Medieval, they probably did rank the first two above the third, but the Greeks may not have, nor the latter half of the Renaissance, nor the nineteenth-century idealists. Indeed romantics of any age hesitate to demote beauty merely because medieval list-makers put it last. To remark on this literary usage, however, is double-edged. There is a very troubling sense in which hope is like beauty: they appeal to the tender-hearted and "sensitive" as sacred; but to the tough and realistic, they are nice; they serve the numerologists' passion for threes over twos, but they simply have no autonomy. As dwellers they are neither nature-born nor invited guest: they are naturalized citizens—the presidency is denied them. Hope and beauty are ephemeral, elusive, too subjective for the realist, too useless for the pragmatists, too derived for the originists. Even for the story-teller the third is a loser: we are born, we live, and we die; stories have a beginning, a middle, and an end. If the greatest is charity, faith comes before the runt of the litter, hope. And yet—

Perhaps this final coupling deserves a firmer foundation. Hope and beauty do seem to belong together in a finer sense. It is this finer sense that needs now to be more avidly considered.

CHAPTER FIVE | The True

Adversities, according to Shakespeare's duke, are like the toad, ugly and venomous on the outside, but carrying in its head the jewel of truth as self-discovery. What is suggested by this wondrous metaphor is itself a gem, or perhaps a whole necklace of precious stones; for the interconnections are a treasury of reflection: without strife provided by the fangs of winter we would not learn the truth of who we are, and such pain enables us to recognize the worth of our own learning. Strife by its essence is, in turn, enabled by hope; but this hope is not a simple desire for a specific victory, that when achieved, discards hope as a mere prop. Rather hope must now be seen as essential for our understanding of truth itself. The rich ambience of gracious gentility in Arden is a concrete manifestation of hope as an existential phenomenon: it shows us what it means to exist as hoping mortals, for whom truth, revealed only to those buffeted by wintry adversity, must matter. This account may seem like a collection of familiar jewels placed in an unfamiliar box. Revered is the wisdom that we must struggle, that truth yields only to the searcher, that self-knowledge is the key virtue of the thinker, that philosophy is an ongoing search. We have heard these things before. What is unusual is to insist that hope should play any role at all, much less the central one. Yet it does not seem entirely random or radical to suggest that the struggle for truth entails hope, for why struggle for anything if the effort is hopeless? Even so, the tradition speaks of the Greek etymology: it is the love of truth, not the hope of it, that sustains.

The seeming disparity between the tradition and the present suggestion is muted somewhat by the realization of semantic overlap: perhaps the love of truth must include hope; or perhaps the species of hope that enables inquiry must contain the lover's passion. This muting has its perils, however; it cannot become a glib convenience. Whatever else hope is, it enables us to learn from what we would otherwise shun; what is loved need not be shunned at all. Indeed, if the analogy is pressed, to speak of loving truth may mislead, for Romeo may climb over the Capulets' walls to get at Juliet, without deeming the walls as dear except as a barrier to be defeated, or as proof of his devotion and agility. The truth-seeker, however, may embrace the strife of his learning as sacred in itself, and hence as disanalogous to the Capulets' walls. If hope enables learning that which, in the absence of hope, is shunned, both the nature of truth as learned and the nature of hope as enabling it deserves reflection. It is not entirely unusual to seek to gain access to the nature of truth by examining the truth seeker, any more than that we might seek to understand love by studying the lover or studying the consumer to comprehend the marketing strategy, or studying the diner to learn the art of the feast. The suggestion then before us is: what can we learn about truth if we approach this topic from human hope?

To seek truth assumes truth is there to be sought. Yet: to dig for treasure need not entail there be treasure. If these are analogous, the first sentence must allow its assumption to be possibly false. But are they analogous? Perhaps we should re-write the first: seeking truth entails there is truth—thus seeking truth is unlike seeking treasure, for I know in advance there must be truth but do not know in advance there must be treasure. We pause: what allows us to say this? Perhaps there is no truth to be found at all. Merely because I seek it does not demand there be truth. Somehow this disturbs: I may not know the truth, or ever discover it, but surely in some sense there must be truth. Is there not a comic irony here: if I learn there is no truth, have I not learned what is true? (Is this what we might mean by "rational hoping"—it is still rational to seek truth that may not be there to find? This ranks "being rational" above and independent of truth, a danger exposed in Plato's Euthydemus.) It is certainly possible I may seek the truth about Atlantis and learn there was no such place; the stories were myths. The only "truth" is the discovery that I was deceived. I may seek to learn the truth about the devil's cunning when there is no devil at all. I may seek philosophical wisdom and learn there is no such thing. This last suggestion jars too violently, though; it does not seem right. I may learn that such wisdom is not what I expected, or that it is not as worthy a thing as I deem it in my search, but can I truly say there is no unknown philosophical truth at all, as I might say of Atlantis?

There is a disanalogy between philosophy and Atlantis, but the nature of it is elusive. We do exist; it is also true that the nature and meaning of our existence can be troubling; but whatever we are, we are not entirely unaware of our existence as meaningful. Philosophers have already revealed to us great insights, we learn from poets and dramatists, musicians and artists. Our search as philosophers does not initiate from some rank ignorance or suspended non-involvement; we carry out an ongoing enterprise that is already rich in both successes and failures. In this, the philosopher is more assured than the searcher for Atlantis. Yet, the inquirer into Atlantis can, in spite of the island's non-existence, still learn. Perhaps from the myths he may learn certain insights into human reality he did not understand before, that are simply independent of whether Atlantis actually exists. Why then is he different than the philosopher who, being human, also holds some false beliefs as true?

The searcher for Atlantis may learn more than that Atlantis does not exist, but his search for Atlantis does not entail that Atlantis actually exists. The thinker searches for philosophical truth; insofar as he learns at all there must be philosophical truth. What is yet more to learn in some sense cannot technically be called knowledge, though that there is more to learn may, in some cases, be called knowledge, as when I know I am not yet sure how to think about mind and body. I not only know I do not know; I also know there is something to know: mind and body are not meaningless terms. The worth of the continued inquiry, therefore, may be unclear, nor can it qualify as knowledge; but it is entirely rational and is not merely one possibility among its opponents. The worth can be over- or under-estimated, but cannot be denied altogether. Thus, philosophical inquiry is not made possible merely because I know some things and am ignorant of others; rather what is known produces a rippling effect beyond knowledge but not exactly ignorance—a sense that my present understanding contains germs of further growth or lures that attract further seeking; lures that themselves cannot be said to be entirely unknown. Great artworks that occur in time, such as drama and music, are often like this: Mozart introduces a theme in an adagio we have not heard before; though we do not know what follows we are curiously familiar as it unfolds, as if we had heard it before—and this in spite of the fact that Mozart always surprises us. Antony's rapture with the Nile's queen prepares us for the tragic end even at first hearing. It is entirely wrong to characterize such anticipatory receptivity as either ignorance or knowledge, but neither is it accountable by the epistemological murk of such feeble notions as guessing, assuming, or leaps of faith. These are milky nostrums that have no curative in them. Philosophical truth, even when grasped, reaches beyond our knowledge, baiting us with lures of further truth, though it is truth unknown but not unfamiliar. We cannot call this familiarity knowledge, nor can we call it ignorance; it is not guessing nor believing, nor is it a mere bridge between our desire to know and our learning what we desired to know. What name, then, can be given? To suggest that the proper title to this curious phenomenon of inquiry is hope cannot, for the reader, itself be unexpected. Speculative naming, of course, is shameless: we can call it whatever we like. However, thoughtful naming is neither entirely speculative nor shameless. Philosophical inquiry is not merely rational, it is also truth-based, and not merely truth-directed; being both is what makes it so troubling. The suggestion here is that what one might call veridic hope is an essential element in the philosopher's fundamental endeavor. To inquire is not only rational, nor is it only truth-seeking, it is also grounded in hope as a dimension of truth itself. This ground is not to be found in the inquirer's personal or subjective make-up; it is to be found in the actual phenomenon of truth happening. Veridic hope is a non-arbitrary, rational, truth-based projection of meaning—"meaning" here is understood as enabling successful thought: what I can think about (with the authority of discovery) is meaningful. Since veridic hope is a projection, we hesitate to call it knowledge; but since it is authoritative and truth-based (not merely "truth-directed"), it cannot be called ignorance. Preparation for this has already been laid out in the chapter on metaxu.

There is a danger in locating veridic hope in the psychological attitude of the inquirer. To speak of the inquirer's "trust" in his reason to lead him rightly toward the proper path, or of his conviction that past successes promises future successes, or that adopting a certain optimism that, in the long run, the rational truth seeker is more likely to discover truth than any other, all may be empirically true in some sense; but such locution is entirely retrograde to the present suggestion. Even the term 'love' is therefore somewhat dangerous, for it seems to imply that some may love truth, others deceit, still others pleasure or beauty. If love is seen as a psychological sentiment within the inquirer, it cannot be equated with what is emerging now as veridic hope.

There is another reason to suggest there is veridic hope. To say that hope enables us to learn from what we would otherwise shun suggests that in the absence of hope certain non-idle inquiries would not take place at all. Why? What dangers are there in being either idle or simply wrong about philosophical speculation? Joy and sorrow, love and rejection, the advance of technology and good mystery books would all still flourish; even moral improvement and social decency are independent of such wisdom. Being wrong in philosophy is akin to being wrong about the ancient Hittites: it seems to make no difference. Why, then, go through the efforts, the concentration, the fierce urgency—all shunnable? We might suggest purely personal answers: some people enjoy doing philosophy just as some enjoy doing crossword puzzles or playing chess. Such endeavors entertain, and are seen to manifest certain cerebral powers, so they also impress. Certainly weaving the fibers of philosophical jargon into vast fabrics of reductionist metaphysics impresses deans and sophomores; doing so can also be rather fun: like the crossword it all seems so neat; when the clues are unraveled all the elements fall into place, and there is satisfaction in the apparent coherence of everything. We do not demand that crossword solutions benefit the world beyond the mere pleasure given to the solver—why expect more from the philosopher? Veridic hope, however, rejects the entire analogy: philosophers are entirely unakin to crossword solvers and those in error about the Hittites because truth matters. To say truth matters as truth and not merely because the knowledge gained by inquiry is useful in some other, practical arena, is to hope in a singular, profound, truth-based way. We must call it hope and not knowledge, for the latter term implies possession, not yearning. Truth matters as truth because who and what we are must matter to a mind capable of self-reflection; who and what we are can never be uncovered by a technique akin to solving crosswords or doing reductionist metaphysics, for once we account for ourselves in terms of a greater plan or world project, our autonomy and independent worth are entirely dismissed, not merely incrementally diminished. Once we realize we are not reducible to schemes, and still recognize the finitude of our knowledge, truth, as distinct from knowledge, emerges as a necessity. What enables this emergence is veridic hope. The phrase 'veridic hope' does not refer to the thinker's hoping there is truth, nor to the trust in certaintist methodologies, but that truth is more than knowledge; and that whatever extends beyond the already known is both rooted in the known even as it widens beyond what is known. If this be true then inquiry is impossible without hope.

What is revealed about the nature of truth if veridic hope is an essential characteristic of the phenomenon? Is truth simply the same as what is the case? Before we dismiss this—and it must ultimately be dismissed—a certain respect for the suggestion is imperative. If I want to know the truth about God or love or loyalty, I want to know if it is the case that God exists and is what I deem him to be; I want to know if what I think about love or loyalty is the case: I do not want to be beguiled by false beliefs. Hence, whatever truth is, it must somehow include this sense of being the case. Or to put it in another way: what I seek in the search for the truth cannot be merely what I would like or what I already believe or what is opined. Much of human error rests on the satisfaction with sentimental appraisals, whether romantically benign or caustically contemptuous. There is a certain toughness in truth-seeking that resists convenient and shoddy acceptance; and it is precisely this toughness that seems on surface reading to uncouple hope from the inquiry, for hope seems to incline us to what is favorable, and if what is the case is not favorable it would seem that hope would distort our ability to grasp it. The toughness inherent in identifying truth with what is the case is not to be seen as a mere codicil of practicality: if I am not robust in my bracketing of sentimentality, I may overlook what is the case and as a consequence suffer more in the long run. If my sentimental hope leads me to trust a scoundrel in spite of evidence, I am a fool and perhaps deserve to be cheated; therefore the advice from such reflection is to make sure my trust is based on what is the case: the scoundrel is not to be trusted. This is eminently prudent; but toughness, in the sense of recognizing that part of truth is simply what is the case, is not restricted to the practical; it is also necessary for philosophical wisdom, perhaps even more so. For in practical matters toughness is often thrust upon us, but in a thinker's inquiry there seems no goad to toughness beyond a respect for learning. What this toughness means, both in its practical and theoretical realms, turns out to be veridic hope itself. The spinning out of fanciful theories—always a danger to the philosopher who would justify his efforts on the basis that he enjoys doing it—lacks toughness precisely because of the absence of hope, not because of its presence. Theories are in a way more lethal than sentiments, because once they are uncoupled to veridic hope—

that truth matters—there is no restraint on the shameless reach of abstractionist speculation. Without this anchor in the concrete—suggested by linking truth to what is the case—there can be no toughness at all.

The toughness, however, remains intact even if we deny truth is merely
what is the case. Most thinkers of various persuasions argue that in order
for there to be truth there must be a reflective consciousness or subject, or
at least a proposition or sentence which then corresponds to what is the
case. The table being set is not the truth of the table being set; yet, neither
is knowing the table is set same as its being true. Whatever is known is
true, but not all that is true is known. More importantly, the love of truth
is not the same as the love of knowledge, though in casual talk the two are
often identified. I certainly can desire to know something without loving
truth, and I can love truth without desiring to know a specific thing. Thus,
although it is important to sequester the toughness that comes from caring
about what is the case, we cannot identify this as truth. Such reflection requires the re-asking of the original question: how must we understand truth
if veridic hope is necessarily a part of what is meant by truth? The answer
is: we must understand truth from the origin of the truth-seeker, and truth-
seeking is a species of fundamental hope. Veridic hope is the rippling beyond what is grasped to that which beckons to a wholeness or completeness;
it is paradoxically the projection toward ultimate coherence. This is a paradox because what enables the projection is itself coherence, yet coherence
is not already known, hence must be projected. I may know that an equi-
lateral triangle cannot be a right triangle; I may also know that all pain is
unwanted, but lovers rejoice in the pain of noble sacrifice; what must be
hoped, for the thinker, is that these two items of knowledge, both true, are
somehow true together; that is, I must hope that I am not two cognitive
subjects, one knowing geometry and another knowing about sacrifice, but
one subject knowing both, and hoping that both somehow belong together
in a wonderful union, even if the synthesis is itself not an object of knowledge but a necessary enabler of self-reflection. To know in two such radically different ways the truth of geometry and the truth of sacrifice cannot
be resolved formally by the mere recognition I am the same thinker in both
cases. That I know both shows me something about myself that is true, but
this showing is not the result of a cognitive act but of a veridic synthesis
that enables them to be thought together: hope. The issue widens by

necessity: there is something remarkable about knowing the truth of sacrifice and the truth of geometry; but this sense of the remarkable is not contained in either cognitive act, but only on reflection of what it means to be able to do both. This remarkable reflection is true, not merely in the sense that I can do both but in the more profound sense that being able to do both reveals what it means to be who I am. The revelation burdens me with the need to think further—but this thinking further both originates in truth and directs itself toward truth, and hence, as hope, is a part of truth, and truth is a part of it.

The danger inherent in the last several paragraphs can no longer be shelved; it may seem the entirely arbitrary nomenclature of hoping is simply part of our limited knowledge coupled to curiosity. Why speak of hope or love when the purely natural instinct for acquisition suffices? Why not simply say: we want to know? Perhaps the philosopher is merely a kitten fascinated by the fluff of thread wafting in the currents of air. Or, if such a metaphor offends, why not suggest in a Kantian fashion that coherence itself lurks as an enthymatic faculty, demanding completeness? Such suggestions have been offered by our greater predecessors, and since they are more formally economical, it seems a violation of Ockham's razor to persist in the present, esoteric reflection. The key term is "formal." Does a consideration of minimalist formality provide enough? Even if we accept such formalist accounting we may still want to know what it means to assume such formal presuppositions. Hope and love may seem dangerously over-affluent, but curiosity and formal conditions may be overly impecunious or even destitute. It is not possible to evaluate these counters without an exile's profane return to the most sacred precincts from which he has been banished by the tyrants of speculation. Like Bolingbroke returning to King Richard's blessed plot, the thinker must confront his liege: we simply must ask more profoundly about truth and inquiry; indeed we must ask about them directly.

We say, without much reflection, such nice things about ourselves: philosophy is the love of truth for its own sake. What can this mean? Is truth for the sake of truth akin to art for the sake of art or science for the sake of science? And even if we rely on the kinship, how reliable are these parallels? There is a surface reading that is surely defensible: art should not be hostage to a political ideology, perhaps not even a religious one: popes and

kings should not tell artists how to paint or even what to paint. (Do we demote the Sistine Chapel because Julius forced Michelangelo's genius to
serve the Church?) We shudder at the banality of much Soviet-era artworks
such as the painting of tractors or power-plants. Science should not be hostage to practical immediacy: the splendid curiosity of pure scientists in a
lab has produced enormous gains perhaps unattainable by labs forced to
search only for marketable products. Yet, even as the thinker recognizes
the need for some autonomy it is not obvious that ars gratia artis or scientia
gratia scientiae should be absolutes. Great artworks have their effect; the
Sistine chapel evokes spirituality in many, as does the Bach Mass in B
Minor. Art for the sake of art has, as an ideological persuasion of its own,
produced some regretful consequences and even worse products; it has even
produced a public contempt for the once-esteemed origins of our greatest
accomplishments. It has also produced an appalling banality in academic
discourse, where art and art-theory become fused and hence confused.
There are good reasons, then, to look askance at such platitudes: perhaps
beauty, sublimity, and passion should return to the genre: the cerebral has
shorter tenure and less warrant than the human; perhaps the ultimate is
ars gratia humanitatis. There are dangers in this; but there are dangers in
any extremist reduction. It is enough for us to be alert to these dangers and
not submit to their banality.

   The comparison is now unsettling. Is veritas gratia veritatis equally
vulnerable? What does it mean to say we love truth for its own sake? The
legitimate appeal to independence in art is that beauty needs no prop, and
in some sense that is true; but though beauty needs no prop it may be that
when beauty is coupled to other things that matter, such as truth and nobility and devotion, it is greater still. If truth for the sake of truth means
the sheer delight taken in knowing, or the mere pleasure that accompanies
the task of inquiry, then perhaps in a very important sense, it is a hostile
doctrine. Hostility to what or whom? Perhaps it is hostile to truth itself.
There is, and should be, delight taken simply in knowing certain things;
but such delight in knowledge cannot be the ultimate justification for seeking to know. Delighting in truth for its own sake, however, may turn out to
be one of two things: either the most dangerous, wicked, and unworthy attitude one can have, or it is the most glorious of all the truths there are:
the truth about truth.

The attitude is dangerous and wicked because it suggests truth is somehow disjoined from reality, rather in the way a photograph of a mountain is not a mountain. To delight in the truth of human struggle with its suffering and its joys may mean to delight in the reflection on suffering and struggle without actually suffering or struggling, and this certainly has its dark side. Perhaps I delight in the truth of human resistance; I am stirred by pictures of death camps or chattel slavery because the endurance by the wretched thrills me with an appreciation of the tough doggedness in the human spirit. In abstracto I then endorse such events, safely removed from their pain, their immorality, their outrage. Is this not a good thing? Or is it a truly wicked thing, for I ought not to embrace degradations of humanity? Ought we to admire the endurance of slaves without also feeling the loathsome disgust at the slave-owner and the vicarious suffering of the slaves themselves? Suppose, in reflection, I speak of the triumph of the human spirit while watching those whom I admire writhe in dire anguish at their lot, and who would curse me for my admiration, crying out: do not admire this reluctant call upon my spirit, curse you! Rather, bend all your efforts to set us free! Is there not a shameful indolence in the love of truth for its own sake when truth contains evils that can be, by effort, amended? Can we endorse the dignity of the slave's endurance without the will to change places with him? What would it mean to say I admire the slave's endurance or even am thrilled at cruel bondage but would not or could not endure the suffering myself? What is this so-called love of the truth that seems to rest upon a voyeur's delight or an abstractionist's safety? This tocsin against the dangers of both artistic and philosophical disengagement is not entirely unwarranted; the reflective, and certainly the speculative, are genuinely perilous; it is self-indulgent to wax romantic about suffering, especially from the comfort of an easy chair. Cognizant of these warnings, however, it is still incumbent to make distinctions that matter: aesthetic judgments are not moral judgments; neither by themselves provide philosophical wisdom. If there is a certain shame at lauding the spirit of endurance without our own suffering there is a further shame in being ashamed of truth for its own sake. What is needed in the face of these disturbing distinctions is a deeper penetration into veridic hope as a synthesis that disjoins as it conjoins, creating a thinkable as well as palpable grasp of what it means for truth to be at all.

One of the more enigmatic, if not downright paradoxical, contributions to this need is Martin Heidegger's insistence that truth, conceived as unconcealment, reveals itself in concealment. This curious teaching has been variously interpreted and criticized; and if there is considerable disagreement about what it means, part of the fault lies in Heidegger's extraordinary reluctance to give us good examples with clear, supporting analyses. Perhaps his reluctance is itself an example of it: by concealing, through his reticence, he reveals what he means. If so, we could wish he were not so clever. Nevertheless, is spite of some irritation at his obfuscatory language, many thinkers find his discoveries to be worthy of serious consideration. Yet, many of his sympathetic critics tend to discuss his analysis without a proper respect for what might be called the genuine problematic, for unless we understand the problem aright we can never understand the resolution aright. Heidegger himself deepened his own appreciation of the problem, so that in later works the emphasis shifted from unconcealment from the hidden to unconcealment as hiddenness. Paradoxically, his finest articulation of thinking on this matter is to be found in his brief essay "On the Origin of the Artwork." For the purpose of the present inquiry, however, it is needful to resurrect the original sense of the profound truth-revealing irony inherent in the problem itself. What then, is the problem?

Heidegger's fundamental concern is to discover what it means to be. The problem is why this should be a problem at all. If there is meaning to our existence should it not be obvious? There are certain phenomena—and Heidegger points this out—in which the occurrence of the phenomenon as an event necessarily carries with it an awareness of what the phenomenon means. Fear, for example, cannot even be unless I know what it means to fear. If I am afraid I know it; I know not only that I am afraid, I also know what it is like to be afraid. The meaning of fear comes with the package, as it were. Such phenomena are unlike external phenomena, for during my first experience with the northern lights, I may not know what it means, since to speak of meanings of external events is to speak of knowing their causes and their effects. But with existential phenomena, to experience the event is to understand what it means to have the experience. I necessarily know what pleasure means when I experience pleasure: these are privileged resources. Accordingly, it would seem that being who I am should not be separable from knowing what it means to be who I am. Rather like

Descartes' Cogito, to think I am means I am, and hence my meaning is already there in my being. How, then, can the meaning of existence not be known? How can there even be a problem? If I were created with a purpose surely I should know what that purpose is; for if I were created with a purpose and not know it, I have been poorly made indeed. Reflection shows that were I to have a purpose I would lose my worth as an autonomous being; and so we remove the servility inherent in "purpose" and replace it with "meaning": if I am constructed, created, or naturally produced so as to be meaningful, surely I must be aware of that meaning as intimately and as immediately as I am aware that I exist. It is obvious, however, that such knowledge or awareness is not at all clear. Why not? This is the problem; and it is a remarkable one, for the problem is that there is a problem at all. This is what Heidegger profoundly considers: how am I to understand, not only my meaning, but why meaning is elusive in the first place.

There seem to be two possible answers. The first is that we create a pseudo-problem: we do not know our meaning simply because there is no meaning. I obviously prefer pleasure to pain, and so the search for pleasure suffices; any "deeper" probing is but misguided musing. I cannot even say I ought to have pleasure or that pain is immoral, for these judgments reach beyond the immediacy of my physical existence and hence physical phenomena. To deny meaning is nihilism; and by its ease it is the most formidable threat to the question since it unjustifies it. The second possibility is that, although the major premise is still true—to exist already contains the muted awareness of what it means to exist—part of our existential construction is designed to impede its realization. Why this is so must, given the acceptance of the first premise, be included among what is impeded by our existential construction. We are, as meaningful, designed so as to keep the explicit grasp of what it means for us to exist in the dark. Early in his quest, in Being and Time, Heidegger designates this existential propensity to veil our meaning, inauthenticity. Thus inauthenticity, particularly in the modality of everydayness, is our original, even "natural" way of existing; authenticity—which means only that meaning is discovered as lurking in the undiscovered—is not at all a natural nor a pure state, but something that can be achieved only through thought and effort. Yet, authenticity and inauthenticity are correlatives: they are valid only in opposition. Unfortunately, Heidegger soon found his terminology itself an impediment, for the terms quickly became bawdy in their use, either as a substitute for moral terms or as supports for any wanton preferences: we, the few enlightened, are authentic; they, the masses, are inauthentic. Indeed, given the date of publication for Being and Time, 1927, the inauthentic sounds like the Marxist's hated "bourgeoisie." The very power of his prose became inimical to his wisdom. In his later works he eschews the terminology, but retains the fundamental insight: we are, in our existential essence, beings whose meaning is necessarily clouded over by our being able to be meaningful at all. This clouding is not total, for the possibility of uncovering it is inherent in the way it is covered. This, however, is the key point of the analysis: what is uncovered cannot ever escape its origin in being covered—indeed to wish it were is to engage in idle romanticism, or what might be called false hope. True hope would be the realization that the uncovered is enabled by the covering in such a way that the covering persists as a part of the uncovering. Existential truth must be found in the concealing inherent in dynamic finitude that, as dynamic, becomes astonished at its limits and thus unconceals. All that lives, dies; but only we realize we die and wonder what it means. Robins and turnips, turtles and sponges live, but their lives are not dynamically finite since they are unaware of their deaths. To be finite is one thing; to know and hence reflect on our finitude seems to surpass finitude: reflecting on our limits places us beyond them; to think reflectively about death and ignorance rather than merely to shun them in panic borrows a shaft of light from the infinite; we become mysterious to ourselves because our very essence is elusive; hope is that existential phenomenon by which we are enabled to find our own finitude mysterious, and in this discovery to find its mystery revealing. Finding our mystery revealing is a magnificent irony enabled by fundamental hope.

Yet, even if we accept these arcane suggestions provisionally, how are we to understand them? Phrases such as dynamic finitude, disclosure in concealment, fundamental hope, and existential truth are not without their own shadows; they do seem promising in a way, but they also seem impish, like the sweet, smudged faces of the achingly vulnerable urchins of the street, apparently innocent; but we dare not trust them; there are far more Artful Dodgers out there than Olivers. There are concrete images that function almost as figures of thought corresponding to figures of speech. We are aware, for example, that disguises often reveal more than the undisguised. The dyed hair of a middle-aged man may reveal his fear of aging, the bluster of a bully may conceal the coward, the pensive gentility of the patient may reveal even as it conceals the promethean fires of hatred. Hamlet tells us one may smile and smile and be a villain; perhaps all villainy smiles—that is, puts on the surface of the friend—else were it not true villainy at all. These are obvious, recognizable ways of human folly that manifest exactly what they would conceal. Such examples may help to the extent we realize that the phrase "revealing in concealment" is not entirely without familiarity. Though they may help, they also imperil, for all such examples tend to be mere fascinating insights into psychological duplicity. The claim here is not that some interesting specimens of human deceit turn out to be revealing of one's inner character; rather the claim is that existential truth as truth reveals in concealment.

The point may be clarified by emphasis. Only as revealing in, and not from concealment is existential truth true. Were it not the fact that my essence is mysterious I would have no essence at all. Only if I am mysterious to myself am I capable of being a human person; whatever I extract as discovery about myself from this mystery requires its shyness and reluctance to be forced out in the open. Yet, this mystery and concealment is not a shibboleth or an impenetrable fog: the efforts of reflective thought are not feckless, progress in the form of wisdom can indeed be made; I am not merely finite but dynamically finite: that is, I struggle both with and against my finitude. The finitude conceals; the struggle with it reveals the very concealing. What is revealed, however, is not merely the fact that I am finite, nor even the more wondrous realization of what it means to be finite, but because of my inquiring, the finitude being denuding not only shames at being denuded, but provokes an erotic-like joy at the disclosure of what would be hidden. Since it is an erotic-like joy at the reluctant disclosure we should and ought to call it a love of truth; but since the disclosure is never quite complete and hence not strictly knowledge it should also be called hope—not hope in the sense of wishing but in the sense of enabling.

Any struggle that is hopeless is meaningless. Essential to the meaning of our existence is the struggle itself; the struggle therefore entails hope; but in this case the hope is not for a mere not-yet advantage, but as an enablement of struggle—that is: a power-giving bestowal inherent in dynamic finitude. This might be called fundamental hope, for it lies at the basis of all particular acts of specific hoping; it is fundamental also because its origin is in the revealing-as-concealing truth of our existential meaning. To speak of struggle as essential for existential truth suggests a powerful disjoining between existential and factual truth. What happens when the meaning of one of the various ways we exist is revealed—even if the revelation emerges out of concealment? Do I then speak of having learned it, and store it along with other items of factual learning in the attic of memory? Or is the very language of knowing that itself an impediment? Can I even be said to know existential truth if such truth is true as manifested in concealing? We say the middle-aged man reveals his fear of aging by concealing the grayness in his hair. Once I realize this, however, I can state a proposition: this man, in dyeing his hair, has shown us he is either ashamed of his age or is engaged in self-deceit, pretending he is younger. These are facts; as facts they are no different than facts known by external experience: I know that product B dyes gray hair. Even if the learning of existential facts is tortured by the convoluted process of extraction from hiddenness, is not the final product the same? I now know the dyer is afraid of being middle-aged. The process of learning the truth is what differs, not the status or reality of the truth itself. Yet—there are no existential facts. If there were existential facts there could not possibly be any impediment barring one person from learning the fact through uncovering and then telling another the same fact merely by putting it in propositional form. Facts—including existential facts if there were any—can always be put in propositional form and always communicated entirely by the form to another who has not had the experience. That is the great and wondrous glory of factual claims: I can tell another how painful it is to touch a hot stove, thereby enabling him to avoid the pain without his having to experience it. Indeed, is not the solid and secure bastion of factual truths of value just because I learn from them what is the case without having to experience them? History is a fine example: I am not nearly old enough to know directly through my own experience what the Civil War was like; but since many who did live through it also wrote down what they experienced, they enabled me to know what happened without my having experienced it. To say existential truth must be experienced in its unfolding is to lose this wonderful advantage of learning from what is written or told. If I cannot tell you, in propositional form, what I learned by extracting meaning from what is concealed, then should it be called truth at all? This suggestion bifurcates truth as learned from the learning of truth, which is entirely retrograde to Heidegger's analysis: truth, for Heidegger, is truth as unconcealing, not the product of the unconcealing. It is a phenomenon. It is not any phenomenon, but that singular phenomenon in which meaning is revealed in—not from—its concealing. Art and language can reveal in this way; particularly artistic language, and chiefly in the species of artistic language we call drama.

Scholars have noted that Shakespeare used Plutarch as a resource for his play Coriolanus. Yet, here is the oddity: in Plutarch's account, every motive for the acts of Coriolanus is scrupulously provided, in order to make the sad but curious tale intelligible. Shakespeare sabotages every single clarification of motive. Why? Without the motives clearly expressed, is not the tale less understandable? Yet the play Coriolanus is a far greater phenomenon of learning than Plutarch. The dramatist conceals the motive in order to reveal the meaning, and hence the existential truth. The more Plutarch provides motive the more I am enabled to judge Coriolanus; the more Shakespeare conceals the motive by suspending the moral judgment, the more I understand the meaning of the tragedy. Perhaps an easier play is Julius Caesar: both Anthony and Brutus, fierce adversaries, are presented as flawed but truly noble men. Anthony's outrage over the body of Caesar is a triumph of dramaturgy: we feel the horror at this ruination of what is splendid. Yet, Brutus's agonizing over his decision to join Cassius's plot to slay Caesar convinces us of the authenticity of his reasons; even Anthony calls Brutus the noblest Roman of them all. The pedant would ask: who is morally justified, Brutus or Caesar; and depending on the answer, the play is then performed according to this moral interpretation. If Brutus is seen as villain, all his lines are seen as indices of weakness and cheap political cunning; but if Brutus is judged favorably because he sought to defend the Republic, Anthony is rendered merely politically astute, and his outrage is but a means of ambition and the lust for power. The playwright struggles mightily to keep such external, moral judgments from taking place at all. The question is not: ought Brutus to have killed Caesar, but: what does it mean for Brutus to agonize over whether he should kill Caesar. The dramatist uses all his skill to forfeit or hide the former question in order to allow the latter question to emerge. Externalist interpretations—all of them— thereby falsify the play. Shakespeare conceals the first question to manifest the second; he hides the externalist morality to reveal the internal drama. Only by this concealing of the externalist can the internal truth of the drama emerge: we learn not which moral judgment to make, but what it means to have to make a moral judgment at all. The latter is a fundamental, existential truth sabotaged by the mere moral concern for the propriety of the act. The tragic artist, then, in order to reveal the greater truth, conceals the external, and in the act of concealing it—as an artistic phenomenon— the meaning of the existential truth—what does it mean to be morally tor- mented—is revealed.

The willingness on the part of the audience to bracket the legitimate but external moral question in order to let the deeper, internal questioning to emerge is a species of fundamental hope. It can be called hope because it accepts truth as prior to knowledge. It can also be called hope since, as is noted earlier, hope enables us to confront what otherwise we would shun— which is precisely the paradox of dramatic tragedy.

This same irony, wondrous in its revelation in the concealed, is found in the greatest of philosophical works, above all but not restricted to, the so-called aporetic dialogues of Plato. The elusive nature of the topic seems to grow as the inquiry develops; definition after definition falls short; as criticisms mount we seem less and less sure of what courage or love, knowl- edge or justice, friendship or virtue, means. Socrates usually ends the dis- cussion with a deprecation of their efforts, saying something along the lines that we are now more confused than ever about what it means to love or know or be courageous. All his analyses seem to produce skeptical fog. Yet few honest readers will deny that the Symposium is one of the greatest re- sources we have in our attempt to understand love; no work in the canon reveals more about knowledge than the Theaetetus; no work available tells us what it means to be just as profoundly as does the Republic; no work tells us about courage as much as the Laches. We learn from these works not merely because they show us inadequate definitions; rather they show us how to think about the topics rather than identify them with labels. Yet, Socrates is not alone in this. Is there anything more mysterious than Kant's antinomies, Hegel's dialectic, Nietzsche's will to power, Heidegger's onto- logical difference? These are not resolutions, since they are darker than what they attempt to explain; yet from them we learn greatly. They, in their profundity, conceal; yet in their concealment, we learn; hence they reveal.

What enables these dark descents into origins is thinking, but it is a thinking that sacrifices ready clarity for the sake of profundity, and such a sacrifice is enabled by a wondrous hope. Fundamental hope reveals by plunging into the darkness, for the bright light of day blinds us. It is a hope wedded to love and courage, but its essence is hoping as thinking. It is not a leap of faith that takes us to the inner irony of truth, but courageous hope. To suffer with hope is to sacrifice; to sacrifice is to suffer joyously. There is the profound paradox; yet in its mystery, in its darkness, all men learn the truth of giving. Hope is therefore a needful companion to those who seek to understand on the level of joyous illumination in a dark place.

CHAPTER SIX |The Dark

Were he but to reach the key, all would be saved. It hung just beyond the barred door, a precious implement of release, waiting for his hand. By extreme effort he could barely touch it, but not enough to grasp it surely. It was his only hope of escape; undeserved ignominy, torture and death were his if the key were not. With huge effort he forced himself to breathe, to relax his muscles, to loosen the ligatures and sinews that, tensed, shortened his reach. As his fingers touched the metal, he knew his only chance was to jar the key loose from its hook and catch it before it fell. Summoning the full battalion of his strength and concentration, he managed to insert the tip of his finger beneath the key; he pushed it upward gently. He heard the jangle against the ring, and grasped for it as it slipped from the hook. The key clanged to the floor, and bounced perniciously away, into another galaxy, as much as an inch: the defeating inch. Within him all seemed to collapse; a dreadful darkness enveloped him, he fell upon the stone and icy floor, damned by his unsuccess. His long, slender, talon-like hands hung curled in anguish from the lowest cross-bar, mute testaments to his forlorn betrayal. Through his veins coursed the chillest current of despair, a seeming liquid darkness quenching light. Turmoil racked him; his unmanly sobs mocking his mysteriously departed courage. What if? If only? Why not a friendlier fall? Another inch? Would he have but tossed it toward himself rather than upward! He now knew that had been the proper method. He was damned by his own folly. This was no mere frustration or passing terror; it set all his inner forces against themselves, like cymbals banging into each other in wanton noise, eclipsing coherence. The ache to reach was yet a feral passion; the sound of the key ringing on the stone floor would not abate; his own doom, like a phantom, mocked him with cruel triumph. Yet his longing did not ebb; it among all the fierce drives and forces seemed dominate, but his poor reason, now racked to distraction, could not abate the promethean furnace of its torture. He wanted; he willed; he ached; he cared; he surrendered; he chided; he sought numbness; he blamed, yet pleaded mishap; for fleeting seconds he even prayed, as if he had forgotten how; he tried to reason but could not. There was a loneliness that seemed to convulse him in self-pity and outrage; he hated his defeat, yet could not summon any strength or wisdom to distance himself from it. He sought death even as he burned for life. But above all he floundered in an appalling darkness that, like a leprous fog, had set the discrete and separate parts of his being into islands, disconnected by the gloom.

He was, perforce, more victim than viewer; but had he been able to re-flect he would know his state as despair; and were he analytic of tempera-ment, he would sense, if not exactly know, that the turmoil of his conflicting states enables a darkness that kept hidden each part of who he was from the others; it was a species of blindness that could not see the parts, and parted, could not see at all. Were he able to reflect—though reflection was precisely that function disenabled by the dark—he would be able to realize the mocking irony that despair is not the absence of hope—for the absence of hope is anesthesia—but rather a species of it; not a non-hope, but an anti-hope; hope working as a traitor to itself. No worthy reflection on hope is possible without due and thoughtful analysis of despair. If it seems a grim and dismal topic, befitting a psychiatrist's office or the darker indul-gence of a European nihilist more than a philosopher's concern, the re-minder must be made that as inquirers we seek to understand what is yet concealed, not to assume, cure, or label. The attempt to grasp the essence is rendered more difficult by the ubiquity of its occurrence in increments. We all experience low-level grades of despair, when a mood of depression follows the frustration of an intensely desired boon. Our deep and fierce love is rejected, and we fall into a state in which all meaningful hope is dashed; a close parent, sibling, friend, or lover dies, and we sink into un-lighted sequestration, feeling no cause nor reason to continue living. An enterprise, built carefully over many years and carrying with it all our dreams, is consumed by flames, dropping our heart into a seeming bottom-less pit. A loneliness, of such ache and tenure that we seem abandoned by all who would be friends, purloins our belonging, leaving us aimless nomads on a wilderness. A child is lost in the uncaring mass of the crowd, and panic looms into the breast of both parent and innocent: the more they seek the greater grows the dread there is nowhere else to look. These are all either kindred to or perhaps lower-level versions of despair; and in most of them we seem to think it is the loss of hope that brings the anguish. It is the brevity of their tenure that confuses the thinker: should such passing woes be clept with such a dire name? Or is despair reserved only for those whose anguish stretches out over unfriendly lengths? Did the mother's panic at losing her child in a crowd reach despair, given that her anguish lasted but half an hour? Was not her immense joy on finding her child a forfeit of that dark appellation; and being so, is it not a distraction to seek in it any clue to understand the sterner sentence? There seems to be a confusion in the project of inquiry. If we seek to find despair only in its rarest, purest form, we may put it out of reach entirely. What worth is there in isolating a phenomenon so infrequent and so unlike any other we can but guess at it by comparison to weaker, possibly kindred experience? It then is the kindred phenomena and not the real thing we must study, and that is a misguided, even foolish, method. If, however, we find real despair thickly scattered around us like leaves in autumn, then is its singularity as the darkest woe not trivialized by the largesse of its availability? This olio of confusion is common to any essential phenomenon that makes up who we are: there are degrees of despair as there are degrees of poverty; perhaps true destitution is rare enough in modern welfare states, but we can be poor enough to learn something of its frustrating meanness and drain of spirit. Our imagination is not so bereft it cannot glean an understanding of the greater from the less. Yet this analogy to poverty is dangerous, for often the difference of degree seems to constitute a difference in kind. True or total despair may entail a certain devastation of spirit not found in the lesser or more fleeting moments; yet such devastation may be discernable as a possibility even in the lesser forms. The hapless prisoner who drops the key may even be saved by some passing hero, and his misery eclipsed after a brief tenure; but his memory can be evoked to remind him what it was like. We are not entirely virginal on this quest.

The suggestion that despair may be a species of anti-hope rather than non-hope now deserves further reflection. The entirely hopeless may well be anaesthetized, even from its own pain. We see them on film or in pictures, or even displayed in art: listless, dull, uncaring zombies, so beaten by the relentless barrage of defeats they stop caring or have the ability to care ripped from them by sheer fatigue. These sad figures seem antipodal to the howling, raging, tortured and fierce image of the prisoner who drops the key. His seems an anti-hope, and its essence is the bewildering pain of spiritual dismemberment. He wants to lack care—a curious irony the bitterness of which is not lost on him. As long as he cares, he hurts; the more he hurts, the more he cares. His passions crash against each other, yet cannot be brought together save in conflict. He endures the lash of worthlessness, yet in his aching he hurts because he cares, and he cares because he would shield his worth. The various elements of his existence are in turmoil; yet they seem all the more isolated and separated from themselves as if they were hurting each other from a distance—perhaps even hurting each other because of distance. Perhaps the essence of despair is this lostness of the self by the self, an inability to bring inner coherence to our various spirited elements. Despair is often accompanied by, or perhaps in part enabled by, a curious species of loneliness. Certainly the prisoner who drops the key senses this profound isolation, cut off from all friends, abandoned to his fate. Yet it may be that the dire loneliness in despair is not the loss of the presence of others, but the loss of our own presence. We are lost not because we do not know where we are; we are lost because we do not know who we are. Perhaps this forgetting who we are is one reason why despair may lead to suicide; death is not seen merely as an end to other miseries, but a mere logical following of our having already lost ourselves anyway. Why live if living needs a whole person and we are just scattered, lonely parts?

We speak perhaps glibly of being a stranger to ourselves; and in some sense this curious self-alienation may simply be endemic of the species, and not a source of despair at all. It is only when this lack of cohesion originates a special kind of torment or intensely personal pain grounded in disintegration of our caring from our finitude. We have not the strength to bring our presence forth, yet neither can we abate the longing to find ourselves, and so we long not to care; our finitude become a cruel mockery of itself. Because we yet long, we cannot say we are entirely non-hoping, for the longing projects onto our finitude; but since, in this state we are absent because disintegrated, and not present, we lack the presence necessary for the project to be ours. It is thus not a lack of hope but an anti-hope: for we hope we cannot hope, we care we cannot care, we long for not longing. Turning hope against itself is singularly pernicious, for in an irony that is most bitter, we trust in nothing outside ourselves, making our own existence the supreme center of the universe, but with our presence disintegrated, there is no center at all, and our abandonment is total.

Never are we more selfish than in despair; yet never is the self more absent. We seek some external redemption that would re-introduce ourselves, but reject that seeking precisely since reliance on external salvation is unbearable due to the screaming pain entailed. To project beyond ourselves in a trust that might redeem is impossible if our presence is also withheld for the same reason. Quite literally we hope not to hope; we scatter our parts all the more widely just because, in recongealing as a unit and a presence, we dread being the target of all the barbs of torment.

This anti-hope can be glimpsed in experiences that are less than total despair. We may hold someone or even some thing as utterly precious, identifying our worth as enabled by its presence. The precious is then lost: at first we feel complete absorption in the pain; we deem all worth has shrunk to the immeasurable; there is no hope. Yet, even as we persist long enough to say there is no hope, we emerge, perversely perhaps, finding our worth at least in enduring the pain. This is despair, but not total or complete; we suffer greatly by the temptations to believe in some remedy or repossession, and know the anguish of rejecting such hopes as cruel. So we, even in this diminished sense, despair, since we hope for non-hope. But the eclipse of our presence, our fragmentation into ever-more bellicose segments that war against each other forfeiting presence altogether, is kept at bay; the ache will slowly heal, for we are still whole, intact. The possibility of the total fragmentation loomed as a dire, and perhaps even briefly desired, possibility; but it is rejected. Perhaps it is even rejected consciously as unworthy of one who would yet endure the pain. For the thinker, this rejection is important, for in its rejection it is recognized. Whether we call it courage or nobility, simple stubbornness of spirit or the intrepid, whether we call it love or hope, rejecting the total fragmentation of our presence into the broken shards of absence is a palpable, enabling phenomenon. Because we can reject the collapse, even as it looms as a possibility with its own lure, we know what it means; and we know what it means not to yield to it. What lures us to yield to the collapse is exactly that phenomenon noted in passing, the anesthesia or numbness of the submissive. The harsh discovery, which may precede the surrender, is that this numbness is not forthcoming, for in submitting to the fragmenting of ourselves we find not a narcotic but a rage, not a costly peace but an internal insurrection, not the balm of the insensate but the even deeper pain of the desperate.

Care must be taken not to dismiss the zombie who lacks all hope. Despair may well have led him to this state of self-retreat; indeed it may be that lurking behind those vacant eyes and listless gaits and pathetic obeisance is yet an ember of the horrific that keeps him subdued. The point is not to classify actual people, but to distinguish existential phenomena. It suffices to realize despair may be anti-hope rather than non-hope; it need not be required to decide who belongs in which category. That there are levels or degrees of despair does not invalidate the distinctions; quite to the contrary, it enables thought in the same way that varying degrees of justice enables us to know what justice is, even if no government or no person is truly, completely just.

The discovery that despair may be anti-hope rather than non-hope can now be seen in light of some earlier reflections. Above all, the pathoempirical analysis of despair as fragmentation of our whole into scabrous and contentious parts gives a new and exciting reading to Kant's account that hope is the gathering or harmony of the faculties. Hope, according to Kant, is an interest of reason in part because it is of the essence of reason: synthesis. On the highest level, what is synthesized are the faculties themselves, and Kant gives the name, hope, to that need to bring the faculties together. The postulates that Kant offers to account for this synthesis, a personal God and an afterlife, are not as fundamental as the enabling synthesis itself: hope. Despair would then be the ultimate impediment to the synthesis among the faculties. If we accept the postulation, it would then also be the ultimate rejection of God and soul.

Far more relevant, however, may be the eerie richness of Heidegger's suggestion that truth reveals in concealment. Despair conceals without revealing; it is the ultimate, radical untruth. That truth can occur in the revelation from or within concealing is a variant account of hope; it may even be the supreme hope, surpassing that assigned by Kant. For if truth reveals in concealment, the finite is rendered dynamic rather than static; the various frustrations we have with ignorance, sin, superstition, failure, and incompleteness become an essential part of our understanding the meaning of existence. This is no limp and ineffectual optionism or giddy lessening of the censures against our errors; it is simply the realization that truth is meaningful, and that meaning is, to some degree, true. If existential truth emerges as disclosure in our own self-concealing, there must be some name we can affix to the will or resoluteness that lets the silence speak or the darkness shine, and 'hope' seems the truest word. Ironies and paradoxes, as resources for truth, must be given enough air and time to arrive at their profundity, and this willful sustaining, or trust in the power or truth to emerge in the gnarls of confusion, is certainly a species of fundamental hope. For the unconcealing of meaning from its hindrances is not inevitable; but neither is it a fantastic superstition built on naiveté. Understanding hope by means of despair is itself an instance of truth-revealing irony that rests on the edifice of fundamental hope.

Mention of the Heideggerian term "resoluteness" brings the inquiry back to more venerable origins. The medieval theologians clept despair as the unforgivable sin. One need not agree with this dire indictment to appreciate the richness of the suggestion: if despair is a sin, it must be the result of some act of will; that is: it must be possible to resist. We are not entirely in control of our feelings, so the mere sentiment of despair alone cannot indict, any more than a soldier can stop fearing merely because his commanding officer tells him not to be afraid. To conquer fear is not to become unafraid, but to become courageous. If it be a sin to despair, the feelings of hopelessness are not what damns me; rather, I am damned by the willful submission to them as the determination of my destiny. For the theologian, doubting God's goodness or even existence need not of itself be sinful; it is rather the complete and total rejection of what it means to be cared about by a personal divinity. If someone very close to me, who loves me deeply and from this love offers a great, sacrificial gift, is then deeply offended by my rejection of both his gift and love, I would be indicted of the most ungracious, mean-spirited ingratitude. Despair for the medieval theologians, is the base rejection of the supreme gift, greater even then the gift of life itself—the gift of a sacrificial redemption. The suffering of the Redeemer was enormous, the warm, gracious love that inspired it was pure; yet the would-be recipient turns away. Put in these theological terms, despair sounds fairly unkind and cruel, a species of rank ingratitude. But it is even worse for the theological mind, for what is denied the personal redeemer is a human soul, so precious a godly presence suffered and died for it; and this suffering bore with it a certain claim or right, at least to be neared; and the rejection of this nearness not only offends the redeemer but destroys the soul the redeemer loves. Thus, they argue, despair unravels the entire weave of redemption itself; it is a total rejection not only of God's goodness but of his loving sacrifice. The sin of despair is not atheism but anti-theism; it does not deny, but rejects, God. Hence it is the supreme sin.

The theological reasoning is not without its own coherence. What troubles is not the theology but the phenomenon. Do we freely act, are we responsible at all, when despair unhinges our hope? If we accept the theological language we must distinguish the mere feeling of despair, which we do not control, from submission to it, which we do or can control. But how are we to understand this? To the prisoner who drops the key, it is the enormity of external circumstances that quenches the flame of hope; bromides to the effect he should keep on hoping for a miracle simply outrage—they come from a Pollyanna pablum of mere flavor and no sustenance, a bright cheer from an empty head. How, defeated in all the props that give credence to his effort, can he be responsible for anything? What could he meaningfully do either way? What act could save, which damn? The theologian might refine by pointing out the prisoner may well lose hope of escaping the cell and the firing squad, but might still recognize the worth of his soul, and not abandon hope in God's redemption. Even if the theological metaphysics may disturb a doubtful mind, the refinement is suggestive: true despair is an act, not an uncontrolled set of feelings, and the nature of this act is a willful rejection. We now must persist: a rejection of what?

If the religious critic is correct, the nature of the rejection is the withdrawal of a radically precious being—a human soul—from a supreme lover who has already sacrificed himself in order to draw near. What enables this rejection is a willful sequestration, not merely from being loved, but from being able to be loved. True despair, as a willful act, is thus rendered morally significant. In the account of the prisoner, however, no mention is made of this possibility. The analysis there focuses solely upon the disintegration of various ways of being who we are, so that we lose our sense of internal cohesion. Such loss of cohesion is the result of psychological trauma and cannot be freely chosen. Is, then, the analysis of the prisoner entirely bereft of any moral content pressed by the medieval theologian? Certainly at first glance it seems the two accounts of despair are simply distinct. We might even suggest that so overwhelming is the prisoner's frustration that his spiritual confusion disenables any free or morally significant act. This first glance, however, can and should be challenged. It is not the feelings of frustration that rack the prisoner, it is the diminishment of his existential worth. Since these effects are in part circumstantial, we cannot deem them "sinful"; but we can see them as lures or temptations. We can call the prisoner's anguish the unopted feeling of despair, which in turn seduces him to seek a false refuge in willing himself unworthy. The nagging of this questioning persists, however; are we not in a dualist's dilemma? If we distinguish the moral act of willful despair from the concrete phenomenon of feeling despair, does not the distinction sunder so severely that the one cannot throw light upon the other? What good does it do to reflect on the feelings if they are entirely disjoined from the act? What good does it do to reflect on the act if it is independent of the feelings? Indeed, if the reflections on the feelings reveal they bring about a desperate confusion, then do not such feelings forfeit, or at least greatly abate, the possibility of responsible agency? It seems, in order to avoid contradiction, we are forced to make a distinction that disenables coherence. Perhaps the theologian and the philosophical inquirer are speaking of two entirely different phenomena and hence have no mutual illumination.

It is indeed tempting to make the distinction and be satisfied with the avoidance of inconsistency. The thoughtful are uneasy at this, however. Both hope and despair are complex phenomena, which means there must be distinctions made; but these complexities are of single phenomena. Is it not possible that what we have been calling the feelings of despair are external manifestations of fundamental despair; and our moral acts toward this existential foundation are enabled by it rather than added to it? The parallel with fear is helpful: in conquering fear we do not stop being afraid, we rather reshape the fear into courage. This analogy suggests that just as courage depends on being afraid, so the "sin" of despair depends on, but is not the same as, the feelings. Even this language is too tepid, however. Courage does not merely "depend" on fear; it is fear—but fear in its noble form. To be courageous is not something other than fear, it is rather fearing well. By analogy, perhaps to despair, as anti-hope, is sinful, but losing hope, when confronted without self-eclipse, can be noble. This nobility is fundamental hope.

In the reflection on the prisoner it was learned that the essential anguish was the chaos wrought by the fractious fracturing of one's integrity or cohesion, leaving us more parted than whole. It may then have seemed that hope was a pre-chaotic state in which the parts were in a peaceful condition of harmony; now, however, with the analogy to courage as fear, we recognize that hope is not the pre-chaotic state but the struggle to achieve coherence in the face of the disintegrating power of despair. There can be no hope, in its fundamental, existential sense, unless there is first the feelings of despair tempting us to a willful act of despair.

It is sometimes noted that children at play radiate hope. This is a judgment rendered by external nostalgia; the young have no need of hope; that is their glory. They may, in some sense, represent our hope; but their very cheerfulness and easy joy are mockeries of the deeper learning that these reflections provide. Children may have keen anticipations for what they desire, and the colloquial usage sanctions the term "hope" in such cases. They suffer intense, though brief, disappointments; but they are incapable of despair as long as their familiar and secure home and family supports them. It is only those for whom the disintegration of meaning is a genuine possibility who can hope fundamentally, just as only those who know true fear can be courageous. It is for this reason that despair should be designated as anti-hope rather than non-hope: the mere absence of hope simply means there are no exits from an impending doom; and though such situations are fairly dreadful they need not affect the person, for the circumstances can still be borne with dignity and courage. Despair, as anti-hope, finds the absence of extrication due not merely to external circumstances, but to a surrender of inner resource to confront oneself, just because the self is split into unconnected parts.

True despair must be contrasted with kindred phenomena that may distract from our understanding. Modern neurological science now recognizes that phenomena such as depression and suicidal tendencies due to a putative loss of self-worth are often the result of chemical imbalance or other entirely physical causes, or physical causes coupled with psychological trauma. On the surface many of these phenomena seem like despair, and common parlance often designates them as such. But chemical depression is an entirely distinctive phenomenon. Many victims of clinical depression confess in their descriptions of symptoms a sense that what burdens them seems alien; they protest their suffering really is an illness, just because their true character is being submerged by physiological origins, not changed by them. Depression, like any other psychological phenomenon such as loneliness, erotic rejection, and failure at an enterprise, may contribute to the external conditions that bring about feelings of despair; but if true despair is also an act in which hope is not lost but rejected, these stimuli to despair-feelings are distinctive, and should not be equated with despair itself. There does not seem to be a willful act of rejection in most cases of depression; indeed many victims of this horrible disease seek out psychological or neurological help in the form of medications, showing that they have not abandoned hope at all; they simply do not know where to anchor it.

It now begins to emerge more clearly why the medieval theologian's assertion that despair is a sin and not an illness is an important suggestion, especially if this act of rejection is wedded to the phenomenological account of the shattering of the self into parts. Both are needed to account for despair as an act of anti-hope rather than non-hope. A second visit to the prisoner may help reveal the importance of joining these two elements. Suppose the prisoner responds to the dropped key exactly as described above. He can find no exit from his dilemma because on the level of external circumstances there are no exits. Furthermore, he can find no inner solace because his internal promptings are disconnected; they clang against each other in discordant cacophony rather than producing a chorus in a resonant key. He thus experiences the feelings of anti-hope or despair. It is anti- hope because the discord of his internal parts actively mute any harmony. Yet, it is possible even now to imagine that, given time, the prisoner might realize that this inner torment is unworthy of himself; he accepts his doom, but does not reject his worth; as a consequence, though he has feelings of genuine despair he himself does not "sin"—he does not act in a moral rejection of his own worth. Under such a scenario, though his feelings are genuinely despairing, he himself does not despair. These reflections suggest, therefore, that any given situation in which a specific hope for a particular boon is denied cannot be the basis of despair; rather despair must alter the person fundamentally in an existential way. The depth of this alteration cannot be accomplished merely by the frustration of particular wants; nor is it sufficient to experience an inner confusion that provides feelings of anti-hope; rather, it must also require the submission of the tormented so that one not only feels but becomes anti-hopes. What is the nature of this submission?

To submit is a morally significant act; it is possible only for a free agent. A free agent cannot decide to become non-free, but can decide to be anti-free. To decide to be anti-free is to hate being a person; it is therefore a passionate, free rejection of what being a person entails. In this rejection, one submits to the lure of supreme disinterest; one opts for an indifference to oneself and to truth in order to avoid the pain involved in caring. To stop caring is possible only by rejecting meaning, so that even the rejection itself is meaningless. This submission is therefore a species of nihilism. Nothing matters. Yet, in order to sustain this rejection, a fierce self-hatred and self-contempt must be re-fueled by the very pain that grounds the attempt to escape being who we are. The irony of nihilistic submission is that the ache of submitting oneself to the supposed narcotic of non-hoping becomes a torment of such intensity it becomes anti-hoping: we hope more and more desperately not to hope. We turn hope against itself just as we turn against ourselves. None hope so fiercely as the despairing. As nihilistic, despair is darkness; what it does not do is cease hoping; for the darkness of despair does not lead us out of the maze, nor does it make the maze disappear simply because we no longer can see it. The darkness merely renders the exits unseen, making us more lost than were we to open our eyes and see. Despair is therefore not only the dark, it is the supremely foolish dark.

CHAPTER SEVEN | The Light

It seems there are two ways to think of light. The first understands light as enabling us to see other things, the way sunlight enables us to see the world during the day, and fluorescent tubes enable us to see others in the office or classroom. In the second way, light is itself seen, as we may stare transfixed before the sinuous flames in a fireplace, or watch the confetti of moonlight skip and scatter on the dancing surface of a lake. It is helpful to designate these two, and I shall call the former "illumination" and the latter "radiance," when the distinction matters. In both senses, hope can be seen metaphorically as light, contrasting to the darkness of despair. As illumination, hope can enable—or provide an essential prop for the possibility of—the management of our spiritual direction, at least by providing links among various existential phenomena that are sundered by our finitude. As radiance, however, hope itself, rather than as a means for some other advantage, can be revered as beautiful or as a source of awe, wonder or worship.

The distinction between illumination and radiance need not be exclusively disjunctive; it is obvious I can stare at the flickering fire in a state of subdued fascination and still use the light to see other things. The present emphasis is on radiance, though in some of the more spectacular instances we discover the radiance in the illumination or the illumination in the radiance. Light as radiant is what enables hope to be beautiful, for beauty has long and often been noted as having no external utility—or as Kant and Schopenhauer put it, having no interest. That we can confront hope not as a psychological prop—that is, having utility—but simply as something worth being confronted in itself, is thus the key to the metaphor of radiance. Yet the metaphor is not entirely aesthetic, for awe, reverence, and worship are also reflected in the figure. Even in the cheap and bawdy appeals of sentimental representations, hope is often depicted as a ray of sunlight beaming through a pewter sky, or the warm light from a welcoming window enticing the passers-by in the night.

It is the mixture of the radiant with the illuminative that the metaphor of light becomes paradoxical. The satisfied, the convinced, the certain, and the happy seem to have no need of hope—indeed for these fortunates perhaps hope is not even possible. The destitute, the beleaguered, the near despairing, the failures, and the wretched, alone need hope—perhaps only for them is hope possible. For these wretches, hope as light beckons first as illumination; but it is often in the unsuccess of the illuminative that they learn of radiance; that is: when the expectations of salvation become so unlikely that reason itself is abused by its reliance, despair may still be bayed by a trust, not in the odds favoring success, but in what it means for there to be light at all. As for the misdelivered package, we become, by being disappointed, grateful not for the gift but for the giving; the light is revered, not used. The paradox then seems to be that we gain hope by losing it. It is akin, though not identical, to the paradox of courage in which the greater the fear the greater the virtue in fearing nobly. Courage too, like hope, can also be beautiful, at least in its manifestation; so that one who does not fear at all can take considerable aesthetic delight in the observation of one who courageously grapples with his fear. This observation on courage enables us to reconsider the happy and contented folk who do not seem to need hope: they do not need its illumination, but even without the need they can revere the light as radiant. If the troubled may begin with hope as illumination and learn its radiance, it is also possible for the grateful, who look upon hope's light as radiance, to learn further illumination; for the radiant may well attune us to new possibilities of nobility and thus provide illumination for achieving it.

By recognizing the radiance of hope's light we can spot the intrinsic worth of the virtue and not merely its extrinsic service toward extrication from the dark. Too often we speak of hope as a psychological crutch that enables us to endure long enough to find redemption from a threatening, external situation. Such a view is entirely utilitarian; for once the redemption or salvation is achieved, hope is then discarded as we toss aside the life-jacket once we are plucked out of the water. The intrinsic worth of hope can never be discovered from the analysis of hope as a psychological prop that urges us on to extricate ourselves from troubles; yet it is admittedly a challenge to see hope as intrinsically worthy. The distinction between illumination and radiance enables this shift to intrinsicality. The light of hope, is, however, still but a metaphor, and needs further analysis.

When we look upon the radiant it is not only the aesthetic pleasure we take in seeing it, we are also somewhat stunned at its bestowal. We can consider, for example, the magnificent presence of war-time leaders whose success depends in part on their mastery of language; Lincoln and Churchill come to mind. We read the Gettysburg address and appreciate its beauty as near-poetic oratory; but we also realize that without him our history and ourselves might well be less meaningful, and in this realization we may recognize an indebtedness or at least a deep sense of gratitude that he was there at all. His oratory obviously played an important role in the Northern victory, and as already noted, it pleases us aesthetically; but in addition, the figure of Lincoln becomes a radiance which makes us wonder why we are so blest to have found him at all. Curiously, the more we learn of his faults and flaws the stronger becomes a sense of reverence, not only for his presence but what it means for us to be his inheritors. For those of a religious bent, the life of a saint may not only serve as a model for living an ethical life but also a source of warmth and welcome into the institutional Church—the first would be illumination, the second radiance. It is only when the life of the saint is presented as the life of a sinner struggling with his sinfulness that his sanctity emerges as a source of warmth and welcome, a point that reinforces the importance of metaxu, but also reveals the intrinsicality of hope. The holiness of the saint radiates out of the disclosure of his presence by means of his story. The discovery of radiance in such figures is always somewhat stunning because there can be no rule, algorithm, or predictability in its occurrence. To speak of these figures as embodiments or manifestations of hope is unstrained: to say that Christ is the hope of the world—and not merely that he gives us hope—is to say his presence radiates welcome and warmth in a stunning (gracious) way. This radiance of his presence is above and beyond the merely moral or even metaphysical; beyond even the beautiful. How, then, are we to understand it?

We can distinguish what we hope for from what we put our hope in. We can put our hope in many things: I put my hope in the steel that gives strength to the bridge, enabling me to hope for reaching the other side safely. I can put my hope in the system of justice, thereby hoping for an acquittal; I can put my hope in the scientific method and thereby hope for the discovery of a cure for cancer. In these cases what we hope in is accounted for by what we hope for. However, there are rather special cases in which our hoping in is not enabled by hoping for; and these cases are those in which we put our hope in a person, as in trust, reliance, love, or worship. When our hope in something relies on hoping for something, the metaphor is of light as illumination; but when we put our hope in someone, the metaphor is pure radiance, for only persons are ends in themselves, and radiance has been provisionally identified as non-purposive. Trust is a subspecies of hope that is akin to the metaphor of radiance, and hence, strictly speaking, to persons only. To trust—or to hope in—someone is a virtue precisely because it is not an automatic or inevitably verified reliance. Were I to know with certainty that a particular person's character would not allow him to purloin my investment, I cannot strictly be said to trust him: to trust means to realize the possibility of abuse; but in trust the basis of reliance exceeds that of possible abuse, often to a rather lofty level. This basis of reliance is the character of the person as radiant: it warms and welcomes as a part of its reliability; but precisely because such trust is a species of hope it cannot be said—nor should we even want it to be said—that it is known as a certainty.

To hope in a person cannot be a mere product of will, as if I were to decide to trust one person rather than another; there must be something in the person that elicits or provokes the hope—which is why we use terms such as awe, reverence, and worship. I do not decide to be in awe of Mozart; his genius compels it—though I can decide never to listen again and hence guard against having to be in awe of it. In this sense hope is not reducible to trust, since I may be compelled to hope due to the greatness of the radiance, but trust, as a sub-species of hope, seems to require my will. The realization of hope being, in some cases, compelled reinforces the intrinsicality suggested by the notion of radiance. But it also suggests something else; namely: there is a power over me that is to be found only in persons, and only in those persons who radiate. The supreme instance of this radiance as power is in the phenomenon of worship, but even in more familiar territory we recognize this in human love. (It is the genius of Christianity to fuse worship and love together.) This realization requires that love not be reduced to or accounted as mere appetite—a requirement that need not be defended here. Worship, even if uncoupled to love, is not of a chosen deity but of an irresistible one. Intellectual theorists may well believe in a chosen deity, but cannot worship such a god. Indeed, nothing more clearly delineates hope from belief—notions often confused or at least over-lapped—than this salient factor: if worship is enabled by hope, and worship is impossible merely for a rationally selected concept of God because hope must be compelled in some sense other than such selection, then hope is not the same as belief, because I can believe in a rationally selected divinity, but may hope only in an irresistible one.

There may seem some variance here. On the one hand we discover that in order to be a virtue, trust cannot be certain; on the other, we learn that a worshiped God cannot be a merely rationally selected divinity. Both trust and worship are enabled by hope; and so it seems hope engenders opposing discoveries. This is not an inconsistency; it merely shows the wide range provided by hope; yet in a curious way this variance is less a widening than a narrowing, a triumph of clarity over vagueness. The realization of how hope differs from faith is a retreat from the vague; but so is the realization that trust, as a virtue, requires an act of commitment, and not, as in worship, an act of submission. Good distinctions, as in noted earlier, must enable synthesis: both trust and worship are enabled by hope, but in trust we em-phasize the willful and in worship the submissive; it is the emphasis that matters, not the exclusion. There is still will in worship and submission in trust.

The realization that trust is a virtue enables certain suggestions to be made concerning the status of its origin, hope. It is possible to classify vir-tues into the tough and the gentle: kindness, tenderness, and tolerance are gentle; courage, loyalty, endurance are tough. We seem to appreciate the former: a gentle youth who comforts others, supports various charities, is quick to forgive, is appalled by violence, and brings cheer by the sweetness of his disposition, contributes much to our sense of what makes the world a better place and life in the world worth living. The tough virtues are more admired than appreciated: loyalties require sacrifice, which is painful; duty is a stern mentor, courage is of the spiritually muscular, and the intrepid have strong spiritual constitutions. The classic virtues seem tough, the newer, enlightened virtues seem sweet and gentle. Compassion is perhaps the greatest of the latter; we deem it one of the single-most contributors to the tolerant and facile freedom that enables modern life to be appreciated by so many. From afar, and with the protection of some historical distance, the tough virtues can be admired without being imitated. Hope may at first glance seem a sweet and gentle virtue, for its metaphoric essence as radiance provides a sense of peace, tranquility, and quiet trust, making us happier. But on reflection, hope emerges as among the toughest of the solid, classic virtues. Loyalty, for example, is the tough progeny of a tougher hope; for the truth of loyalty is not service to be rewarded but service inherent in a bond; it is the offering of one's reliability in a manner independent of lure and consequence. Hope is much more akin to courage than to tolerance or gentility. Indeed, for the sensitive and the gentle, loyalty may seem a harsh impediment to the achievement of a cheerful, charitable existence. The difference may be more readily grasped by comparing tough and gentle virtues that seem to have similar consequences. To a friend in trouble, the gentle virtue of compassion may lead us to efforts that would help extricate him from the perils that threaten. To a friend in trouble, the tough virtue of loyalty may lead us to summon all our resources to extract him from his dilemma. Since both virtues result in our helping the friend, how are we to understand the difference? Compassion, by its etymology is rooted in our ability to feel the same, or at least associate, distress; and since we ourselves would not want to be unaided in such cases, we feel the promptings to provide assistance. The loyal, however, do not rely on such sentiment; rather, in a self-awareness that is almost a species of pride, the ligatures that bind us to the friend suffice to provoke an awareness of duty: it is being a friend that matters; it is not that the friend's torment causes us distress. Compassion would have us provide assistance because we share his pain, loyalty would have us provide assistance because he is our friend. One may, of course, help the friend from both compassion and loyalty, but when loyalty is the central motive, there is a toughness of spirit; when compassion is the central motive, there is a tenderness of spirit. Though the truly virtuous may have both, it does not keep us from the distinction.

Hope is a virtue of the tough in part because it enables sacrificial worship. This worship is not a mere recognition of existence nor is it a commercial act as when we perform rituals in order to gain personal, theological benefits. Instead, worship grounded in hope rather than mere belief accepts burdens and even personal suffering or loss surely on the basis of the magnificence of the divine presence. Such worship is not the calculation of interest but the instinct to revere; it reveres not out of simple fear but wonder.

It is with this declension that we realize the full meaning of the tough version of worship.

What would we be were wonder to be lacking? Since wonder, in addition to providing a recognition that something is worthwhile, also thrills us with the sheer, gratuitous magnificence that it is there in its worth, to lack wonder would require our assessment of worth without the thrill of being overpowered by the radiance of it. The assessment would be the result of calculation, whereas the wonder would be instilled as a passion. Since wonder, reverence, and awe all seem passions of submission it may seem they are enabled by the virtues of gentility; but it is rather the toughness of hope that generates them, for it is a glorious paradox that awe and wonder strengthen rather than weaken, just as an erotic but deep love, while turning us to malleable pudding on the plate of the beloved, emboldens us to drastic if sometime comic strength and giddy valor, providing a meaty and energetic sustenance. Perhaps it is the very toughness that makes us so very gentle.

The distinction between tough and gentle virtues is not entirely benign: there are dangers in it for both species. The first peril is that the tough are admired through the dissembling filter of nostalgia: we look back at the virile golden age and find there the glory lost by a softer, milkier present. Such nostalgia is not only unworthy, it is also blind; if hope be tough, part of its toughness is persistence, and so it is still with us. The counter danger is to dismiss the tough as outworn remnants of male supremacy and the false glorification of war and power. Tough does not mean feral, crude, dominant, or cocky. Neither does gentility imply the weak nor compassion a mere sentiment. The language here must itself be tough and gentle: we speak of virtues, and accordingly must be strong in their defense, seeking, as philosophers, the truth, and such seeking may require the toughest fibers in all human action; yet the truth-seeker cannot dismiss the gentle, sensitive refining of our vulnerabilities. It does not take long for one to wonder if the tough are really gentle and the gentle are really tough, and hence the distinction itself falters. The point of distinguishing between them is, however, too valuable to dismiss. It is a meaningful thing to suggest that hope is a tough rather than a gentle virtue, even if we must scatter like plentiful condiments all the caveats over the entire dish. It is what we learn about hope that matters, and the distinction, even if braced by caveats, props our understanding. We do not hope as weak, we hope as strong.

The radiant metaphor of the fire in the hearth or the lighted window in the storm-splashed night reveals what might be the penultimate discovery of hope as light: welcome. To suggest that hope welcomes is not, however, a mere further characteristic that is added on like ells to a building: it changes the fundamental nature of existential metaphysics, for with it we cannot think of ourselves as mere quanta or pluralistic entities that just happen to occur in an indifferent cosmic container called the world. Rather, we can dwell or abide in the world as a home if welcomed, or flounder as outcasts from the world if not. The bases of dwelling and its opposite, exile, are not sentiments within subjects, but essential ways of thinking about who we are as opposed to what kind of entities we are. Such thinking alters profoundly the very meaning of the world—an ancient and revered topic in itself. What is the world? Is it an entity that happens to contain other entities, among which are thinkers; or is it a dwelling, from which we can be banished in exile or welcomed as belonging? Or is "the world" merely a covering phrase that equates with everything that exists? To decide among the various alternative ways of thinking what the world is cannot ever begin an inquiry, but only develop in the unfolding of argument. If welcome is enabled by hope as radiant, the phenomenon itself must first be considered with some depth.

Whatever else welcome is, it simply cannot be conceived as inevitable; it must in some sense be granted or bestowed. Yet, neither is welcome entirely arbitrary; children have certain claims to belonging simply because they are ours, as do in-laws, to a lesser degree. Exile seems to demand justification: we cannot dismiss family members on whim; but aliens must be distinguished from family else the words themselves lose all meaning. Aliens are not the same as exiles; it is the latter who are genuinely unwelcomed; the one-time alien, as new in-law, can be welcomed into the family, even if not personally liked or favored. The suitor or would-be in-law however, has no right or claim until accepted; but even the rejected suitor is not an exile; the latter is rejected as unwelcome, the former is merely denied the original welcoming. Even the in-law, however, is not automatically welcomed, for the family may reject him as unworthy, though such rejection may alienate the daughter so that she, in effect, exiles as unwelcome her parental family.

The term 'exile' may seem quaint to the modern ear; for many intellectuals the threat is entirely toothless, first because it is now almost impossible to exile a native-born citizen for any reason, and secondly because the exodus to another country seems insignificant. An American might feel entirely at home in any English-speaking country—visiting Canada or England does not jar, so why should moving there permanently matter? Yet it does not take much imagination to feel the possible loss: to be unwelcome where one belongs can, for many, devastate; to be indifferent to exile may mark the banished as profoundly lacking in a quality that seems essential for a worthy existence. Exile is not a mere absence from a place, but a rejection of our belonging; it disjoins us from the welcome that enables us to share in the origin of local values and customs; but most of all, if we borrow from the light metaphor, we are left out in the dark and cold. In exile we are denied the enclosure of belonging and thus denied hope.

To the lost wanderer who shivers in the black, wet night on perilous terrain, the discovery of a lighted window beckons cozily and warmly; when the knock at the door is greeted by the words, 'come in; you are welcome here,' the feelings of gratitude and relief seem overwhelming. It is then we realize that the light from the window initiates the welcome, as if it were put there for the sake of the lost. To see the light and not be welcomed is mockery; so that the beckoning is not merely a prelude to, but an essential part of, welcome, and hence of hope. To be able to hope makes welcome possible; light as radiance is a metaphor of hope in part because of its beckoning welcome, in which we are given entrance to dwelling. If we are not merely in the world as coffee is in the cup, but dwell in it, to be in the world is to belong in the world. To be able to dwell and to belong at all is thus grounded in hope. As light, hope radiates welcome, inviting us to belong; in its absence there would be neither welcome nor belonging, and the world then would simply become a container. Since being a container cannot describe what the world means, without hope there is no world at all, there are only items or entities; by this reduction we ourselves become only items or entities. It is thus hope that enables the thinker to reject the metaphysical illusion that we are mere items; hope as radiance provides truth. From these insights gained from the penultimate offering of hope as light, we now are able to turn to the final discovery.

The ultimate truth manifested in the metaphor of hope as light is that as radiance it has its own intrinsic attraction. It is better to hope than not to hope, even or especially when, in a state of contentment or bliss, no particular boon is hoped for. If all our wants are, however briefly, satisfied, we do not hope for anything, but we can continue to hope in someone. We can appreciate this quality in another as we might appreciate the physical beauty or natural grace of one who is dear; but we can also rejoice in our own hope as radiant which becomes, as an inner light, part of the spirit that enables us to realize we matter independently of our success at any specific endeavor. In this special sense, however, to say we matter beyond our success requires the addendum: to whom. It is entirely possible to suggest that in one sense our mattering beyond our success is simply a quality or characteristic of our own existence as worthy, and hence not dependent on any other person, and we might speak of "mattering" because of rights or because of the dignity inherent in being a human person. In hope, however, this notion is amplified by the addition of mattering to another. In Christian theology, for example, it is argued that we matter beyond our success because we matter as beloved children to a divine father in whom we place our hope. But even if we are chary of such theology, we can say we matter to those who love us, as with parents, children, friends, and spouses; and because of such mattering, we find we put our hope in them, thereby discovering it is better to hope than not.

These present reflections rely upon the metaphoric wealth of light as radiant; as metaphor, however, it has limits, and cannot of itself suffice beyond the richness of its suggestions. As long as this caveat is kept in mind, no harm follows from such a metaphor; indeed, much is gained. For by means of the metaphor we realize that hope itself, and not the benefits promised by the hoping, is a worthy thing. It is better to hope than not; and this is no mere psychological boon; it is rather a truth learned by reflecting on what it means to be a person. It is with this discovery, however, that the inquiry no longer can rely solely on the metaphor. It is precisely because hope in a person is so distinctive that a new irony now emerges. What, we must now ask, is inherent in being a person, that allows for hope to be placed in us? We not only put our hope in others, we must also realize others can put their hope in us. What do we learn from this inversion?

CHAPTER EIGHT | The Inversion

The first heart-stung youth informs us of his giddy plight. He speaks of his trembling and ache; how he longs in the long hours of her absence; how in his addled confusion, he can neither eat nor sleep; how his tongue is first an organ of golden eloquence and then, upon the passing of but a minute halved, is thickly glued to the dome of his now treacle-thick maw, leaving him stupidly mute. We hear of all the comic suffering, the rapid shifts from promethean desert to arctic waste; from Himalayan heights to the oceanic depth of Marianas; from dark remorse at being born, to splendid confidence in his unconditioned worth; he envies all others than himself; he is the envied, yet, of all. We nod and smile and say, ah, yes; he loves. The second youth has words only of her: how radiant she is, how sweet her smile, how every item of her story is a verse in the epic of wonder. She purloins all other wealth, becoming the exchequer for each endorsement. Pure she may be, yet feral in her carnal lure. Her virtue shames the saint, her pulse measures the cadence of all music, her tongue outspeaks the poets'. Did you know her eye is lashed with black and silkened curls? Mark how she helps the infirm—why delay her canonization, even for a day? Do you painters not see the arch of her foot is the arch of the firmament? Do you teachers not see the origin of all learning in her wisdom? That stone, there, is now a shrine, all you who know what worship is, for she, the holiest, once sat upon it in brief fatigue, making weariness itself a sacrament. Are you all blind? Do you not see her? Ah, we say, he too, loves, nodding as we smile, amused and tolerant.

Yet, the difference is at first curious, and then, on reflection, profound and then disturbing. The first speaks only of himself, the second only of his beloved. Who loves the more? Are not true lovers those who focus on whom they love? Perhaps we might suggest the first is in love with loving, the second in love with his beloved. Yet, this seems too severe a judgment; the first must truly love to be so addled. The question itself seems to unsettle even us who smile and condescend. Why is the second, second? Surely this is not the only reflection on what now seems to emerge as a deeper problem, requiring troubling thought, and not mere reaction. So deep an asking must have greater historical precedents.

Readers of Plato's Symposium may note that when it comes time for the youthful Agathon to deliver his speech on the praise of love, a fundamental shift occurs that prepares the way for Socrates' dialectic. Agathon rightly protests that the first four speakers have all addressed the nature of Eros solely from the perspective of the lover, leaving unconsidered the very ground and reason for loving at all, namely the beauty of the beloved. Perhaps this is because Agathon himself is young and beautiful, and hence beloved; but in any event it does seem a little odd to conduct a symposium on the praise of Eros without serious consideration of both beauty itself and the beloved. His praise of the beloved prompts the deeper reflections by Socrates; but even on its own, Agathon's speech echoes as a warning against approaching so rich and intimate a phenomenon without including what enables it in the first place. Yet, this reference to the Symposium is more than a mere insistence that the beloved should be included; for Agathon chides the older speakers; he does not merely correct their errors. Indeed he scolds them as the young always scold the old in matters of the heart: they must have forgotten what it is to love.

Perhaps we need an Agathon-like reminder to shame us who ask about hope only from the need of the ones who hope. For the needful who place their hope in a savior, it is not those who hope but those in whom hope is placed that matters. The victims plucked from the angry flood praise the intrepid rescuers, urging a plaque to honor these heroes, not to honor those saved. What does it mean to say we inquire into hope and leave out what enables hope at all: the one in whom we hope. Is the analogy to the Symposium a valid one? If so, we cannot resist noting that in the dialogue the first four do indeed speak of the lover, suggesting that perhaps it is somehow fitting that, dramatically at least, we must ask first about the lover, for that is easier to ask; and only then can we reach the deeper asking about the beloved; perhaps then it is dialogically necessary to proceed as we have, asking first about those in need who hope, and only at the end to ask about the one in whom hope is placed. Even were this valid, the further question now must be raised: is there wisdom or distraction in making an analogy, not between this inquiry and Plato's dialogue, but between the actual phenomena, love and hope, themselves? For this is a disturbing realization: not all analogies serve the truth; it may be a disservice to push the figure. Yet these early reflections seem to promise at least a further if not deeper insight into hope. Analogies cannot be pre-judged; they must, like all philosophical suggestions, be allowed to unfold; the warning perhaps suffices: if we learn something, it is worth it; we simply must be alert to the possibility that the analogy is dangerous. The precise nature of it needs reiteration: the point is not simply to compare hope with love, but hope, as grounded in the trusted rather than the trusting, compared to love, grounded in the beloved rather than the lover.

If Agathon deserves our thanks for his Copernican revolution, centering the universe of passion on the sun of the beloved rather than on the earth of the lover, a further revolution, which promises much for the analogy with hope, must now be entered. The poets and panegyrists are not so naive as to praise only requited love; they know that the rack of unanswered passions often tortures the lover to howl out the secrets of his greater slavery. What they rarely do, however, is to sing of the peculiar anguish of the beloved who does not, perhaps cannot, requite.

Suppose we are deeply loved by one whom we do not or cannot love in return. We may sympathize with the other, perhaps even tolerate to some extent the need, but simply because someone loves me does not require that I love in return. If the lover presses the suit beyond tolerance, the beloved may be forced to a genuine distress or even disgust, and must either yield in pretension or seem cruel in rejection. The burden of being a non-requiting beloved can, for the sensitive and charitable, be agonizing. Especially for those who themselves are vulnerable to the dire ache of an unanswered love, to be loved erotically by one who cannot be loved is embarrassing and burdensome: we do not want to curse the loving, for that is unfair; but even to curse the lover seems harsh. To pity the unanswered lover may be unseemly; there are times when the only resource is harsh denial, and even if warranted, such necessity simply cannot please: we wish profoundly not to be loved in this way and by this person. Why is the non-loving beloved of interest? It is the analogy with hope that warrants the focus on this almost overlooked figure. Perhaps Agathon's heliocentric revolution opens the gate to the inversion: what does it mean to be a reluctant basis for another's hope? It may be we should consider first the uneager before the eager, lest in spotting the latter we confuse the eagerness with the responsibility. If someone puts their hope in me, I can regret or rejoice in it; if I regret it, the yet-abiding trust is revealed in its unadorned and awful purity. The seasoned general, veteran of many campaigns, falls in action, and the command is passed to the green, reluctant young officer. The men are forced by the chain of rank to place their hope in his unseasoned command; he is forced, now entirely uneager, to take up the crushing burden of being the basis of their hope. It is not always so; we could select a joyous father's realization that he is the hope of his adoring children. Indeed, for this inquiry to be complete, it is requisite that the second figure should indeed be a willing model. The inquiry itself, however, following the discoveries and the analogy must imitate this reflection with the reluctant. Yet, it is not the green officer that offers the richest analysis of the unwilling, nor is the happy father the richest for the willing. The reluctant juror and the passionate mentor offer more. These two shall be followed by the worshiped; and only after the reflections on these three will it be possible to judge whether the Agathon-like inversion applies successfully to hope.

The reluctant juror is both a paradox and an irony. We speak loosely of putting our trust or hope in the judicial system, and this looseness of argot deeply deceives, for a system is precisely that in which no hope can be placed at all. We can rely on a system, but hope only in persons in it. Abstractionist dissembling once more misleads us, with dire consequences. Whether we like it or not, in a criminal case brought before a jury trial, the people of the state must, perforce, put their hope as trust in the actual, personal, living, and flawed juror; and the juror, especially if he is reluctant, as many are, must accept, perforce, the role of being the basis for the people's hope. The system is merely that which provides the structure for placing our hope in the juror. Not all jurors are reluctant, of course; but some are, and it is precisely those who now must be studied as the basis of our hope.

If I, as impaneled, reluct to serve, it is in part due to the comprehension of an unopted authority: I may not be wise enough to know with certainty whether the defendant is guilty or innocent, but this lack of knowledge does not excuse: I simply must judge. This judgment, however, is not a mere guess or opinion: I must assume a certain authority I may not deserve, but it is authority nonetheless. This point must be stressed: the authority is there whether I want it or not; it is there whether I warrant it or not; it is there whether I am justified in having it. Hope bridges this gap between my non-desert and the public necessity. But what is it about me that enables this hope to bridge what, merely on my powers, I could not bridge? We note first that those involved in the actual crime and its resolution, such as the victims and their immediate kin, the accused and his kin, the police, the prosecutorial agents and counsel for the defense, are by definition partisan. They are so strongly identified with their own preference that the system begs for an uninvolved non-partisan, lest the judgment be distorted by the pathos of intimacy. Further, we note that the juror is asked not only to evaluate the evidence, but to make judgments: in common-law countries the jury is required to find the defendant guilty only if such guilt is shown beyond a reasonable doubt—though what constitutes reasonable doubt is itself determined by each juror. The juror is thus not required to be omniscient, but only to be reasonable in his judgment. Here, though, is the crux: no judge can instruct the jury what 'reasonable doubt' means, in part because no one, not even logic professors, can instruct one how to be reasonable. What would it mean for someone to be able to instruct me on how to reason? Good logic teachers can point out the dangers of bad inferences, but each time they do so, they appeal to my own being reasonable as the basis for my grasping it. A freshman may assume that if the sentence "some apples are red" is true, he may infer that "some apples are not red"; the logician points out a case where such inference is unwarranted, and the student realizes that his own reasoning is self-corrective. Being told the inference is invalid does not insert the power of reasoning into the student's head; it merely wakens the slumbering powers of logical discernment already there.

If this seems to belabor unduly the obvious, it is because the point is crucial to understanding the hope placed in the juror. We trust him in part because he, like us, is not only reasonable but able to discern, by interior reflection, what being reasonable means. Unlike the logic student, however, the juror is not concerned with the mere forms of reason, which can be codified into neat decision procedures, but with the reality of being reasonable, which must include—as logic cannot—the dread realization of our human frailty. To doubt reasonably requires doubt and reason—and what a droll wedding is contained in this union! I am asked to push doubt to the very edge or brink of being reasonable. It is precisely at this point, this brink of reason, that I must doubt the authority of my own reasoning, not in the sense of abandoning it but in the sense of testing it. I can invert the question: "is my doubt reasonable?" to "is my reason doubtable?" I must ask not: "what are the rules of inference?" but "what are the limits, revealed by thinking, to my trust and mistrust?" It is in part because I can trust and mistrust the testimonies of two conflicting witnesses, that I can be trusted as juror. Hope is placed in me because, as a finite person, I too can hope. Even as reluctant—or perhaps especially as reluctant—I can be the basis of my fellow citizens' hope, because as finite reasoner, I too must hope, and be able to hope. It is not formal reason alone, but doubting and trusting, that enables me to be a less than omniscient judge that nevertheless has authority, even unwanted.

Yet, the realization of my finitude, which is part of the ground for my reluctance, is insufficient to explain this inversion of hope. I also must care about justice: I hesitate to find the innocent guilty, but I also hesitate to leave unpunished and at large a dangerous felon. The people of the state trust me, even if forced, because I, too, am a citizen. As trusted, I become their representative, their deputy, their ambassador as caring members of a civil union. It is, however, not any civil union, but this one. Their trust in me is therefore not merely as a finite, rational person, nor even as one concerned for justice, nor even as a member of any civil union, but as a sharer in our union. Indeed, when examined, my very reluctance is not based merely on my cognitive shortcomings wedded to the need to pass judgment, but perhaps more deeply because I may fail as the object of this hope placed in me on the basis of our sharing. It is, then, not merely the already serious matter of justice, but the deeper ligatures of belonging that intensify my reluctance even as they also intensify what it means to be the object of my fellows' hope. This realization needs an intuitive support. Suppose I, as a juror, support by my vote a verdict which later evidence shows to be false. Though I may regret the error, my fellow citizens need not censure me if the evidence was fairly strong in support of the original, though false, verdict. If, however, they learn I had been suborned, especially if the subornation was venal, the sentiment against me is not simply one of anger or frustration, but of betrayal. They feel, rightly, betrayed. But betrayal is

possible only on the basis of an intimate trust. There is no betrayal if the
legal agents of another country are suborned: we may be outraged or
shocked or sad, but not betrayed. This suggests that hope, in the special
sense of hoping in someone, must pre-exist and enable betrayal. It is only
because Washington trusted Benedict Arnold that his treachery reached
the level of historical condemnation; it is because Judas was loved and Brutus trusted that they reside in Dante's lowest level of the Inferno.

If we now can suggest that, by being the object of another's hope, we
can betray, and that betrayal necessitates the prior phenomenon of hoping,
we begin to see the bonus of wisdom in the analogy to the Agathon-like
inversion. To be able to betray, though to remain loyal, is now revealed as
a key discovery in the existential meaning of being the basis of another's
hope. Such trust and its consequent loyalty, however, require a species of
intimacy, as family members are intimate, or tribal, and then perhaps even
communal, members are intimate. They understand who they are in part
by their membership; violations of this belonging are betrayals, not mere
crimes. Such intimacy alone enables one to be the basis of another's hope.
If this suggestion is to hold, however, we must distinguish the basis of hope
as intimate from mere opportunistic hoping. Caught on the roof of a burn-
ing building I spy a helicopter approaching with a dangling rope: I do not
care whether the rescuers are locals or foreign or even aliens from another
planet: I simply want to be saved; and it seems I must put my hope in those
who are in the helicopter. In this case, however, the loose language misdi-
rects: I hope for the rescue, and hoping in follows from the hoping for; that
is: there is no residual meaning to hope beyond that of being rescued,
though sentiments of gratitude and relief may follow from it. The opportunistic is therefore originally hoping for, not hoping in. Indeed, if the rescue were afforded by entirely natural events, such as a steel beam falling
across the roof providing a bridge to the non-burning neighboring building,
my hoping for would be answered without the need for any hoping in. We
can, however, hope in reluctant jurors; and we can, as reluctant jurors, realize what it means to be the basis of others putting their hope in us. The
latter requires the intimacy of belonging that enables betrayal and loyalty.
It must be stressed that the present reflection on the juror is not the moral
one resting on the juror's duty, even if duty is more basic than the loyalty.
It is morally wrong for a juror to vote on the basis of his prejudices or his

greed if bribed; but the moral integrity of the juror which would keep him from such wrongs is assumed, not hoped. Loyalty in this sense is the loyalty of intimacy and belonging, not individual moral rectitude. This reflection on the reluctant juror suggests that what must be existentially presupposed about someone in order for him to be the basis of another's hope, is the loyalty inherent in belonging, enabled by the intimacy of sharing, and the realization of authority based on judgment rather than knowledge. Since I am capable of such existential qualities I must endure the burden of reluctant acceptance of being the hope of others. The understanding of what hope means is incomplete in the absence of realizing what enables us to be the hope of those with whom we share belonging. Just as Agathon insists the praise of Eros is incomplete without grasping the role of the beloved, so we now are prepared to suggest our inquiry into hope must include some sense of what it means to be the hope of our fellows. Once we realize the nature of the intimacy and sharing, however, we also must grasp the comparison of hope with love is not merely analogic: the loyalty of affection and not mere duty provides the anchorage to our being the hope of others. I cannot, then, be required to be the hope of all others, but only of those with whom I share an intimacy of belonging. I may be morally required to assist a drowning person; this duty allows the victim to hope for relief; but to be one in whom hope is placed requires a loyalty of belonging and not a mere loyalty of duty.

It was not that long ago that the mentor was deemed an admirable figure. Socrates was the mentor of Plato, Washington the mentor of Hamilton, Wagner was briefly but intensely the mentor of Nietzsche, Hayden to Beethoven, Pershing to Eisenhower. In the contemporary current of mistrust, however, mentors are increasingly unwelcome: not only are they seen as threatening the independence of mind in the learner, the very relationship between mentor and student is deemed unhealthy, on various levels of dark unease. Our present culture shamelessly supports the psychological counselor who induces false memory of abuse and creates a dependence of the most slavish and sordid kind; but frowns puritanically on the wondrous intimacy of those who share learning with joy. In spite of this climate of murky suspicion, however, luckily or perhaps gratefully for the courage it takes, there are and probably ever will be true mentors in whom those eager for learning place a very special species of hope that is singularly verdant in promise. From it we can learn about hope what may be unreachable by any other avenue. It may be Agathon's inversion at its radiant best.

What is a mentor? The word is often used in the context of teaching or counseling, though curiously neither the instructor in a classroom nor the advisor in his office should be identified by the term. Rather, the image is closer to that of a seasoned veteran in a guild, guiding an apprentice, or of a wise confidant personally involved with the young learner over a period of time. The Oxford English Dictionary offers its first definition of the common noun as a trusted counselor, reinforcing the notion that a species of hope is placed in the mentor. The educator or teacher in a classroom has an obligation to each of the students as well as to the class as such, but the mentor is usually seen as one person concernfully guiding one other, usually younger, in a way that surpasses what is found in a lecture hall. Although we can be mentors to more than one person, each relationship is seen in terms of one-on-one. Very often the term suggests a fondness between the two, or at the very least an intimacy based upon the sharing not only of what is learned but the joy of learning itself. It is this very uniqueness or privilege that so irritates the modern critic but also provides the relationship with its greatest charm: the learner is favored, select, precious, and even elite. The mentor may be drawn to his favorite originally on the basis of the young learner's gifts and promise; but as they develop, their respect for each other takes on a personal fondness rooted in their mutual love of truth and of the beauty and virtue in their inheritance. They delight in each other's delight, so that the guidance of the more mature seems entirely unobtrusive. To some extent, the trust by the student in the mentor must be earned; and this earning is in part accomplished by showing the worth of things by sharing the pleasure taken in them. It is precisely this shared joy in the wider, existential erudition, that requires a certain sense of privilege or favor: yet it is a favoring selection that enhances both. This puts a lie to the puritanic critic who darkly judges the mentor as taking delight in and perhaps even abusing his power. This is a deceived judgment because whatever power there may be is shared rather than kept; there is no arrogant puffing up of one's importance or esteem because the mentor impresses the learner with the authority inherent in his erudition. There is authority: but it is authority shared; conversely, too: there is admiration; but it is also admiration shared. That is the whole point of mentorship: the guide seeks to share the worth of learning with the guided, and the guided seeks to share the joy of such learning with the guide. Indeed, as shall be suggested, the very hope placed in the mentor ultimately mirrors a hope placed in the learner. This can only happen on the basis of a favor, since not to favor at all is an insult to the natural gifts of the learner and the natural admiration of the learner for the one who recognizes and celebrates them, as well as the joyous recognition of the gifts in the discernment by the mentor. Why not favor the gifted?

It is in being selected or favored that the singular species of hope is to be found. The mentor cares about the learner becoming worthy of what is learned, the learner puts his hope in the mentor as trust-worthy as a model of learning. The nature of this hope is deeply paradoxical, in part because it entails a submission to be led, which seems passive; but the leading is to autonomy, which seems active. It is a dependence that enables independence; the more intimate and private the sharing, the more universal and liberating its achievement. The focus here, however, is not on the learner's hoping, but on the mentor's being the eager hope of the learner. There may be reluctant mentors just as there may be eager jurors; but for the sake of this inquiry we are asking what it means to be an eager, non-reluctant, mentor. The eagerness is remarkably singular: the mentor cares about this particular learner, not all learners; as eager he takes joy in being the hope of this one learner; and this happens to each favorite if one is mentor to several.

The paradigm may well be Socrates as we see him in several aporetic dialogues. This is not the Socrates of the Apology appealing to the Athenian citizenry; perhaps not even the Socrates of the Sophist, in which the characters are subordinate to the emerging theoretical account. It is, though, very much the Socrates of the Charmides and Lysis, the Ion, Euthydemus and the Phaedrus, in all of which the palpable fondness of Socrates for the youths to whom he speaks is as essential to the dialogue as the arguments or disclosures. Yet it is the very fondness in these dialogues that makes Socrates as mentor suspect, for one can gainsay the eroticism inherent in them only at the cost of self-deception. In spite of this danger, however, these dialogues are simply too rich to be dismissed altogether. In what sense is Socrates, as mentor, the hope of his young listeners?

The temptation to answer this quickly or glibly must be resisted. There

are obvious factors: Socrates is wise in the sense he knows of his own ignorance; he is artful in his craft, in the sense he knows how to elicit from
the youth his own critical sense of ignorance; he offers insights into what
truly matters, such as the virtues, the nature of reasoning, and being a good
Athenian; he not only tells them things, he shows them things; his own
being virtuous is often a resource for learning what the virtue means. Yet
admirable as all these qualities are they do not spot the nature of the hope,
and so we ask further. It may be worthwhile to ask in whom the youths do
not put their hope. They have learned that the sophists, though promising
much, do not deserve their hope. This mistrust in earlier teachers, however,
has not left them convinced they can learn from no one. Learning from
Socrates, that both he and they are yet ignorant, they still hope, for they
also learn they cannot by themselves inquire as deeply as they can with
him.

Socrates bids them to think along with him; he does not, as some mod-
erns do, bid them to think on their own, for not even Socrates can do that.
Here is the first spark. Perhaps they hope in Socrates just because he hopes
in them. Neither he nor they can put such hope in themselves, for hoping
in oneself can be shown to be impossible or at least perverse. Socrates does
hope in these young men; and perhaps this hope in them is impossible
without his love for them; but in any event their hope in him is echoed,
and perhaps enabled by, his hope in them. He truly learns by talking with,
rather than merely to, the young. He is wiser than they, but cannot inquire
without them; and so he puts his hope in them; and it is because of this
that they put greater hope in him. This suggestion needs some refining and
support.

Why suggest one cannot hope in oneself? To find in oneself the basis
of "hope" is to deny the essence of hope, for hope, like love when properly
considered, depends upon another. In the vernacular argot we sometimes
hear that one puts his hope solely in one's own will or achievement; but
this says little more than that one relies on oneself for the courage and determination to achieve what one deems worthy accomplishments. Such
strength of character can be admired up to a point, but to characterize it as
hope unravels the essence of hope, and discounts by one the number of virtues. We do not need fewer virtues, but more. If such courage and determination are virtues it does not follow there are no others. Part of the

persuasion to anchor hope in our own will is rooted in the plerophory of the last two centuries that anything and everything of value is within us; we simply do not need another. Love and hope, however, as well as piety, are virtues only because we do need others. It is indeed possible for someone to deem oneself sufficient, and hence rely on no one else, but such a move is less rather than more virtuous. It is a variation of the earlier analysis of false hope in which the grieving father assumes all power to restore his son's health, and becomes a monster. The same point can be made with the twin, love. We speak of self-love not as a virtue but as a vice: strictly self-love is a misnomer, for self-love is simply self-interest, and all the meaningful things about love, such as sacrifice, dependence, and comic folly, are lacking. If hope does indeed require another in whom we put our trust, the closest we can get to "self-hope" is in reciprocal hope. The mentor exemplifies this. The young men of Athens put their hope in Socrates partly because he puts his hope in them; they trust him with affection because he is wise, but also because he has affection for them and their emerging wisdom.

The true mentor not only delights in sharing the joy of learning, he is also burdened by the realization that, as mentor, his own character infuses learning with a concrete sense of what it means to learn. The dread realization of scandal thus becomes a check upon his own interests. Scandal is to behavior as confusion is to learning: they both roil and dislocate. Bacon has pointed out that confusion is a far greater evil to the inquirer than simple error: we can learn from our mistakes but never from our confusion. Scandal roils the conscience: simple human weakness may lead us to act against what we know is improper, especially when the lure of temptation is strong and sudden; but in such lamentable lapses we still realize what we ought to do. In scandal, however, our reliance on anything and everything is upset, we founder as in a tossing sea; no learning can occur because we are buffeted by the whirlwinds of confusion. If Bacon is right that cognitive confusion is worse than error, Jesus is right in condemning as among the worst of sins, scandal, for scandal purloins trust, and with it the hope in all possible guardians. Almost by definition, the mentor is the paradigm of one who can scandalize. Merely by being trusted, the mentor may find himself behaving more nobly than were he not trusted, for the realization of the dire virus of scandal burdens, and license is girded. He is forced to become, by the hope put in him, a better man than he would otherwise be. This is a moral advantage in being a mentor; but it is also a burden. Why accept this burden? There are two reasons: the first is because the joy of sharing wisdom is greater than the distress of the burden. The second is that without mentors, those who matter to us—the young learners—are bereft: they cannot hope. Do we mentor those we first love; or love those we come to mentor? In Socrates' case, it seems more frequently to be the latter, though in some instances the reverse occurs. With Lysis he clearly becomes a friend to and finds a friend in, the boy because he first shares philosophical inquiry with him; with Charmides he first is stirred by the brief peek inside the boy's garment, and then launches into the inquiry. With both boys, however, the actual inquiry itself seems an aphrodisiac: sharing inquiry is, in these dialogues, an arousal. This can be read either metaphorically or literally, depending on how uncomfortable it makes us, but in either case the love is seen as a good thing, not a bad one. The point is greater than the image: we accept the burden of being a mentor because the joy of sharing the inquiry and the moral obligation to provide models outweigh the cost.

It is a peculiarity of the joy in sharing learning that it is reciprocal; the suggestion here is that not only are the joy and the learning shared, but so must be the hope. The boys and young men put their hope in Socrates as mentor, but Socrates also puts his hope in them in two ways: first they become the reservoirs of virtue as the potential leaders of the next generation; but second and more importantly: they offer the joyous companionship in the shared search for truth. Yet, for all the coziness and intimacy this suggests, the reciprocation does not reach to mentoring itself: Socrates alone is the mentor; the young learners are not. Though they may both put their hope in each other, the nature of the hope is not the same. Socrates can scandalize them; they do not scandalize Socrates. By sharing the inquiry with them, this mentor mirrors their trust in him by his own trust in them; but the hope placed in the mentor is the original that the other mirrors. It is curiously the reverse of the love: Socrates loves the younger Phaedrus, but the dialogue bearing his name shows us the younger's is an echoing love to the older's. Socrates may be loved, but he is always the lover first and originally; Socrates may put his hope in the young men, but they are the original ones who hope.

Being the mentor of the young, with all its dangers, is a joyous life. Socrates, as a paradigm of the mentor, not only lives but dies joyously; and the reason is not merely because he loves truth but because, as mentor, he is the hope of the young who would learn from him both his joy and his wisdom. He loves not only the truth, but also the fellow truth-seeker; because of that he not only is trusted by those who put their hope in him, he also trusts, putting his hope in them. We learn from this something profound: being the basis of hope can be mirrored. Further, we also learn: we can learn from the reflection in the mirror.

It is because we can learn from mirrored reflection that we can interrogate the final figure in whom we hope, namely: the one in whom we hope as worshiped. Since we must ask this question in terms of what it means to be worshiped in a manner that entails being the basis of the worshipers' hope, it would seem supreme arrogance to ask it at all. Not being God, how can I know what it means to be worshiped; surely as finite I can only know what it means to worship. Yet, even as we consider this, the analogy to love offers a handhold, and in two senses. The closest approximation we have to worship of the divine is the metaphor of the lover worshiping the beloved. Juliet says of Romeo that he is the god of her idolatry, and Socrates assures the eponymous Phaedrus that lovers would fall on their knees and worship the beloved were it not for the shame involved. In the same dialogue we are provided with the metaphor of the streams of beauty entering the eyes of the beloved wherein most are absorbed, causing his wings to grow by which he can soar to the height of truth; but some bounce from the beloved back to the lover, providing him with a counter-love or echoing passion of the original. If love can provide an echo of itself, why not worship?

This point is not that arcane. To say we put our hope in a god whom we worship, and mean but this that the hope is an essential part of the worship, enables us to reflect on what it is about the worshiped that accounts for his being the basis of our hope. Whatever else we mean by the word "hope" we cannot mean assured or guaranteed reliance: I do not hope two and three add up to five, I am sure of it. Conversely, I cannot hope two and three will one day, after the revolution, add up to six, for I am sure it cannot. To be the basis of another's hope as worshiped entails, then, some sense of trust as opposed to certainty, and indeed only as a trust in a person who bestows or endows, not an automatic machine that inevitably dispenses.

If Romeo is the god of Juliet's idolatry, one way to understand this is to see Juliet as offering herself to him in a way that entails her willing to be mastered by him as an erotic lover. Her virginity matters to her—she would not surrender it to anyone except her husband, for two reasons: she feels she would be cheapened were she to be wanton prior to her marriage—that is: Romeo may love her less ardently if she were not virginal. But also, she is virginal because of her own self-esteem and pride: being pure matters to her. Yet, this concern for her virginity conflicts with her own erotic passion: she strongly desires intimacy with Romeo regardless of any feelings about marriage, virginity, or custom. To idolize him as a god entails her eagerness to be taken and mastered, as if his desiring her somehow dominates all of her hesitancy and desire. That he be satisfied ranks above her own satisfaction. There are similar conflicts in Romeo's love for her. The metaphor of erotic worship suggests that such worship is not debasing: Juliet does not feel less worthy for her idolatry, but more. The metaphor with the erotic cannot be allowed to mislead. Worship is usually understood as a ritual, in which the religious community is united in its sacramental adoration of our god, not merely my god. Private prayer is not worship, nor is the reverence and belief toward an individually conceived deity. To be the basis of hope as worshiped therefore entails some sense of favoring and belonging; the worshiped, even if divine, thus participates in a reciprocal relation of loyalty and trust, the violations of which are not merely immoral but special treacheries called sins, or more profound betrayals called sacrileges. In Christianity, the reciprocity by the worshiped is understood as redemption or salvation, however conceived. To be the hope of the worshiping community thus requires the worshiped to be able to save. This ability is not merely enabled as a possibility by the acts of worship, but enabled as an actuality by an act that must be concrete (i.e., historical): an act of redemption, conceived not as an automatic or inevitable phenomenon, but as a bestowed one—not entirely unlike Juliet bestowing her virginity to Romeo; that is: yielding it. The very nature of the worship is thereby altered, for it now, as a publicly shared ritual must also include gratitude for this sacrificial, bestowing act. To be the basis of worshipers' hope is thus to be a savior, with all that implies, including being able to be thanked. Yet, this emphasis to salvation easily distracts from the earlier discovery of intrinsicality. Worshipers do not merely hope for salvation—though their ritual may originate in such sentiment—but they also hope in the worshiped, regardless of the benefits that may follow. The extent to which this hoping in—which establishes the autonomy or intrinsicality of hope—dominates to the point at which hoping for fades out or even vanishes, is sanctity. Few may reach this state; but as a possibility it beckons.

The worshiped, whether a divinity or a beloved, is thus a paradigm for fundamentality in being the basis of hope. The appeal to the divine is not meant to argue for the metaphysical legitimacy of any theology, but simply to provide a supreme model of what it means to be hoped in: only in this way can hope be seen as having intrinsic worth, for my hope in the beloved or god outlasts and out-reaches my hoping for anything. Perhaps no human being can ever be comfortable being worshiped in this way without being arrogant; as finite persons, however, we have some sense of why it matters to be able to be so esteemed. Great courage may be necessary to accept this possibility about ourselves; either that or great arrogance. To realize the enormity of this courage suffices to show what being worshiped means.

Fundamental hope is intrinsic. No mere opportunistic hope can ever be raised to this level; but hoping in persons can. The analogy with Agathon's inversion offers this discovery by our reflection on being trusted as a juror or joyously sharing wisdom as a mentor. When fundamentality is pressed, the idea of a worshiped divinity being the basis of our hope is mirrored in the beloved being adored to the point of worship. Fundamental hope is therefore revealed as entirely intrinsic, and is found only in hoping in rather than hoping for; indeed its essence as fundamental is achieved only when we hope in a person without linking it to hoping for any benefit to ourselves. Akin to the beauty of the beloved, it needs no external justification.

We are hoping beings. Hope lurks in our sharing, in our loving, in our thinking, in our expectations, and in our finitude. It is not a mere sentiment or optimistic attitude, but pervades throughout our being; even despair hopes. It is both an act and an existential necessity; in some species of its manifestation it enables spirit, and when celebrated it becomes a rite. It binds us together; yet it individualizes. Yet, for all its rank, it receives little or no respect from most thinkers; and when they do try to understand it, the majority see it either as a formal, enabling faculty, or they ladle upon it sugary treacle and cheap sentiment, treating it as a psychological buttress for the sagging spirit. It is perhaps all the more powerful for its being missed by the surveyors of the human landscape; it persists as an essential quality within us even as we disparage it by inattention or misinterpretation. Yet, for all its shyness, it provokes inquiry for those who attend to its subtle voice. Truth itself requires it; to seek the truth about truth is so sacred to those who think, that to leave this wondrous phenomenon unasked and unconsidered is shameful. We hope to avoid this shame.